A TOURIST
in My Own Life

For Fathers Who Yearn For
A Deeper Relationship With Their Children

RICHARD J. DANIELS

Stonebrook Publishing
Saint Louis, Missouri

A STONEBROOK PUBLISHING BOOK

Library of Congress Control Number: 2017952668

ISBN: 978-0-9830800-9-1

www.stonebrookpublishing.net

PRINTED IN THE UNITED STATES OF AMERICA

10 9 8 7 6 5 4 3 2 1

A Tourist in My Own Life is a deep, introspective look at fathering. Rich turns personal trials into powerful testimonies. His humor and humility grounded in hope encourage readers to self-assess and aspire for greater familial connection.

F. Willis Johnson
Senior Pastor, Wellspring Church, Ferguson, Missouri
Author, Holding Up Your Corner

Rich Daniels's concept of being a tourist in your own life is a powerful metaphor. Through it, Rich wakes us up and guides us to make loving and spiritual connections with our family, our friends, and the new faces that cross our paths every day.

Mark Uhlenberg, MEd
President, The Heartwood Group, LLC,
Saint Louis, Missouri

In this book, Rich shares how easy it is to be the father you want to be for your kids. His honesty and his heartfelt stories inspired me to choose to engage with my two boys daily. As a member of the same men's group, I have received encouragement and hope, shared ideas and exchanged stories with other fathers who long to love and know their children. Thanks to Rich, I continue to find ways to love my children for who they are and to make sure that they know they are loved each and every day.

Thomas Richter
Account Executive/Designer, The Graphics Company,
Saint Louis, Missouri

Don't be intimidated by Rich's awesome dedication to building a relationship with his kids and making a lasting difference in their lives. Instead, be inspired to take a first step to making a difference in your kids' lives today.

Mike Fischer
Retired CEO, Peak Performance Business Solutions,
Saint Louis, Missouri

A Tourist in My Own Life captures the transparent heart of Rich Daniels—a father who opens up about fatherhood and its challenges. Taking a humble look inward, Rich discovers the painful reality of not being a fully present father. Determined to reform, he does the necessary work to establish strong relationships with his children so they feel known, valued, and loved. Rich's dedication—and his success—are a huge inspiration to fathers!

Paul Robinson
Founder and Pastor, Kingdom State University,
Saint Louis, Missouri

Living life with passion and an engaging smile helped Rich Daniels succeed as an athlete and entrepreneur but didn't guarantee him success as a dad or seamless relationships with his children. To fathers who yearn for deeper, more meaningful relationships with their children, I heartily recommend *A Tourist in My Own Life*, which describes Rich's journey as he learned to connect with his kids in a Godly way.

Eric Cope
Founder, Smile Squared,
Saint Louis, Missouri

I've run with Rich for many years and enjoyed our authentic, sharing conversations during our runs together. For me, reading this book was like being on one of those runs with Rich. Enjoy!

Russ Kuttenkuler
Executive Director, JSI, Saint Louis, Missouri

This book is for my father, Mike Daniels, who showed me what it means to be a father of faith and family, and who sacrificed everything for his children. I also dedicate this book to my wife, Megan, and to our three beautiful children—Grace, Luc, and Zoey—who make me want to be a better father every day. I love you each as you are perfectly made and thank you for loving me as your earthly father—even with all my shortcomings.

Special thanks to my book coach and friend, Nancy L. Erickson, The Book Professor, who encouraged me, inspired me, and taught and coached me every step of the way to make this book a reality.

I would also like to thank my friend and spiritual mentor, Pastor David "Padre" Bennett for grabbing a cup of coffee with me the day after Christmas where we kicked off our first men's group. Thanks to my mother, Sheila, my brothers, Mike, Brendan, and Greg and my sister, Patty, for showing me what family really means. Lastly, I want to thank all the men in my men's groups from Saint Louis, Missouri; to Macomb, Michigan; to Brussels, Belgium; to Mount Olive, New Jersey who have shared their inspiring stories and testimonies, challenges and struggles, joys and frustrations—all in the spirit of encouraging one another to be better fathers and brothers.

A TOURIST
in My Own Life

*For Fathers Who Yearn For
A Deeper Relationship With Their Children*

CONTENTS

FOREWORD

Who among us has not been a tourist in his or her own life? Authentically living in the moment is a wonderful idea, but it's difficult to achieve. The challenges of trying to be successful and balancing a professional and personal life in today's world often lead us to become tourists who stand at an emotional distance and simply observe our interactions with those we love.

Have you been living the life of a tourist? Have your day-to-day interactions become transactional interchanges of "this for that" that diminish authentic relationships?

Tourists have a tendency to stand at an emotional distance and simply observe those they love. And when stressful situations emerge, tourists protect their feelings and preserve their emotional energy, avoiding personal involvement. But being tourists in our own lives—rather than proactive, involved, passionate participants—steals the very life that awaits us and that can lead to tremendous happiness and fulfillment.

How do you become present in the everyday moments and relationships of your life? How do you prevent the busyness of your life from distancing you from those you love the most and who can bring true meaning to your life?

In these pages, Rich Daniels courageously reveals the personal challenges of being a tourist in his own life that he overcame to "come home and move in." Rich confesses that he once was satisfied with having people *around* his life, but that they were not actually *in* his life. And he boldly reveals his struggle to "live into" each day by authentically relating to those whom he loves.

I'm privileged to be Rich's pastor. His family affectionately calls me Padre, a name that I cherish. I'm proud of the courageous personal journey that Rich has taken and that he has chosen to share his journey with others so they also can discover increased value and meaning in their lives.

Many say that the most important thing in any relationship is to authentically know those you love—not just to know about them, but to know them. The Hebrew word for this is *yada*. But included in this ancient idea is the profound wisdom that you must allow others to know you as well, which requires personal vulnerability.

Dear tourist, the bold, risk-taking invitation you are about to discover in this book is based on the incredible grace of God, who loves and accepts you just as you are—and even loves you so much that He will be with you to empower you to come home and move into your life.

In one sense, we are all travelers through this life. But the Gospel of Jesus Christ teaches us that there is more. May you take up residence in the relationships that mean the most to you. May you risk knowing and being known by those you love. May you know that God is inviting you to unpack your luggage and come home.

Padre
Rev. David Bennett

PREFACE

I have a confession to make. If you bought this book to discover the formula for raising your children the right way, you'll be disappointed. I don't have all the answers. In fact, I've probably made more mistakes as a husband and father than many other men. My three children have borne the brunt of my mistakes. My hope, however, is that you'll find something in the story of my successes and setbacks that will feel authentic and ring true for you—at a minimum, a tip or an approach that will give you a measure of hope or a light in the darkness.

———

I've often grieved the loss of the dreams I had for each of my children when I was a young father. In fact, I've often denied even having these dreams because they felt so superficial: that my kids would be straight-A students, amazing singers or musicians, star athletes, winners in an important arena. But my dreams for them were more about their performance and achievement than about my being in a healthy relationship with each of them.

I used to get mad and yell at my kids for their child-like shortcomings. For example, if I saw that they had special gifts—like becoming a talented athlete—but they didn't work at developing these gifts, I thought they were being irresponsible, Then one summer I read *The Matheny Manifesto* by Mike Matheny, and I resolved not to yell anymore when I went to my kids' athletic events. You can't imagine how hard this was for a guy who grew up in New York and yelled at the TV during every sporting event.

Once I'd decided to stop yelling, I asked my son after one of his games, "How did I do today, Luc?"

"Pretty good, Dad," he replied. Luc's assessment convinced me that I was indeed capable of change.

When my older daughter, Grace, was in her freshman year in high school, there was definitely a change going on with her. She spent more time alone, it became harder to get her up for school, and she became a "fan girl"—obsessed with certain shows and celebrities to the point that it interfered with her daily life and responsibilities. She not only binge-watched these shows with her friends on Netflix or Hulu, but she also was a fan of the stars on social media and sent hundreds of memes to her friends.

My parents would never have accepted this behavior, so neither did I. There were many times when I told Grace to "suck it up" and get going. I held her to firm boundaries and strict consequences, playing the role of disciplinarian, scolder, punisher, and enforcer. Turns out, Grace was suffering from anxiety and depression. And as she was reaching out to me for emotional help, I was pushing her away with my "suck-it-up" mantra.

The advice of a good friend helped me—and Grace—get through this very difficult time. My friend told me, "Remember,

Rich, they are God's children first; we are simply their earthly stewards."

I'd never thought my children belonged to God first, nor had I viewed myself as a steward of those precious lives. My friend's comment forever changed the way I viewed my role as a father, and it helped me change my relationship with each of my kids. I've become much more aware of my children's thoughts, actions, and behaviors, and I share my observations with my wife and kids before I take action. I'm surprised at how often my initial interpretation is wrong.

—⟨⟩—

Our three children—Grace, Luc, and Zoey—share the same genetic makeup and the same upbringing. But each of them has a unique set of abilities, a unique temperament, and a unique personality. They don't *feel* the same things and don't *need* the same things. As their dad, my job is to make each of them feel known, valued, and loved.

When I finally set my intention to be the best dad I could be for each of our kids—to stop being a tourist in my own life—life in our household got pretty exciting. But first, I had to confront the excuses I'd hidden behind. And I had to take action to remove the barriers that kept me from connecting with each of our children in a way that was meaningful to *them*.

As you read this book, I hope you discover something new about yourself, find a new vibrance in your relationships with your children, and embrace your role as a steward of those precious lives, so that each of them feels known, valued, and loved. May you find hope and inspiration in these pages, laughter and camaraderie in the stories, and freedom in knowing that you're not alone.

A TOURIST IN MY OWN LIFE

One crisp spring morning, I felt pretty strong on my usual hour-long run with my buddies. As we crisscrossed through our small suburban town, we passed perfectly manicured lawns that surrounded storybook houses. After awhile, we encountered another group of runners heading toward us.

One of the guys in the group recognized me and said to the guy on his right, "That's Megan's husband."

The guy's friend then shouted at me, "Hey, Megan's husband."

Wincing, I hollered after him, "I go by Rich now."

Being known as Megan's husband is a joy and a gift—in fact, it's my secret plan to get into heaven. I've often fantasized telling St. Peter, "I'm with her. I'm Megan's husband." But I wanted to be known for myself, and I made a mental note that maybe I should take time to get to know these people in my own right.

A few months later, I went to a school program for one of our children. Everyone knew my wife, and she seemed to know everyone. People literally buzzed around her. I said "hello" to faces that were somewhat familiar, but I realized how little I actually knew about any of them.

1

Later that fall, as I walked down the hall at church to pick up our younger daughter, Zoey, from Sunday school, I had the same experience. The other parents looked familiar—I'd brushed up against them for months—but I didn't know any of their names. A question began to haunt me: Was I satisfied that people were *around* my life but not actually *in* it?

It suddenly struck me: I was a tourist in my own life. Like someone on vacation, I liked to be friendly with the locals, but I wouldn't dare get close to them or let any of them in. Although I had some good friends, I had little depth outside of these relationships. I was a great employee, colleague, and supervisor, but when it came to my own home and community, I was simply a tourist who was passing through to enjoy the sights, not interested enough to contribute anything that lasted. Was this the legacy I wanted to leave?

I started thinking about how confident I felt in my business life—and how starkly it contrasted with my skills as a dad. In my business, I've always been intentional about growing and learning, taking part in executive coaching sessions at top B-schools and hiring expert consultants when I needed advice. But I didn't apply the same rigor or methods when it came to my family. If other people saw me as "Megan's husband," how did my kids see me?

When kids are little, they love it when their dad is around to play games, read to them, swim together, wrestle, whatever. And if your children are well behaved and compliant, you may enjoy this role for years; relationships are easy when things are going smoothly. But when you face challenges and lack boundaries or guidelines for the children, the consequences you impose often appear harsh to them and produce the complete opposite of the desired behavior.

I saw that I lacked know-how as a father in several areas. The first was obvious when I returned home from one of my frequent overseas business trips. I didn't know how to reconnect with my family—and didn't even know their established schedule. As a runner, I knew very well what it felt like to be out of cadence with my stride. When I reentered the world of my family after an absence, I felt the same way: out of synch with my family's rhythm.

A friend had once cautioned me not to disrupt my family when I returned home, so I didn't. But that made me feel like I didn't belong. I decided that I didn't want to feel like a disruptive tourist or an unwelcome guest in my own home anymore. But I lacked the presence and, I admitted to myself, the patience to be in real relationships with my wife and kids. What I needed to do was learn to listen to each of them and to share their joys and concerns, their hopes and fears.

My inadequacy was again evident when the kids either started a new activity or learned something in school a different way than I'd been taught. For example, I had no ability to help Grace learn music or sing, which she wanted desperately to do. I'd once sung "Happy Birthday" to a friend of mine and then overheard someone else ask who was singing so off key!

I also lacked the skills to teach my children properly. I tried to teach one of my daughters math the way I'd learned it, and she said, "Dad, that's not how my teacher taught us." It turned out that this inadequacy wasn't that hard to remedy. I went to a parent night at school where we were taught the new math strategies, so we could help our kids at home.

Finally, I couldn't be objective with my kids, which hampered my ability to be an effective teacher. When I tried to teach Luc to play baseball—to throw, catch, hit, and field a ball—we both became frustrated. Luc didn't want me to see him struggle as he learned; and it was frustrating for me because Luc wouldn't listen to my instructions and didn't get it right the first time.

A wise pastor friend once told me that our children might not want us to see *them* fail because they'd never seen *us* fail. And, I realized, we'd never shown them how to properly deal with failure.

One time I got angry with Luc over something small, overreacted, and raised my voice—OK, I yelled at him. My ugly New Yorker came out in full force. Remembering what my pastor friend had said, I went to Luc, kneeled down to his eye level, and said, "I'm sorry, buddy. I shouldn't have yelled at you. Please forgive me."

I needed to do this a lot more.

————❧❧❧————

My feelings of inadequacy as a father eventually led me to seek help from others. I wanted my identity to include being a father who knew, valued, and loved my children. And I wanted my children to *feel* those things to their core.

Here's a story that has had a profound impact on me:

One Thanksgiving, a father and son walked around the property that surrounded their home in the country to burn off the feast they'd just eaten. The young man turned to his father and asked, "Dad, when will I be a man?"

The father walked on and thought about how best to respond. When they turned a corner on the path, he pointed to a large boulder and said, "When you're able to move that boulder is when you'll be a man."

The son ran to the boulder, tried with all his might to move it, but failed. Every year, when the father and son took their annual Thanksgiving walk, the boy tried to move the boulder. But the boulder wouldn't budge.

Finally, the year came when the boy was as tall as his father. He'd spent the summer throwing bales of hay in the fields, and he was certain that this, finally, was the year when he'd move the boulder. The son gave everything he had, but the boulder still didn't move an inch.

In frustration, the son turned to his father and said, "Can you help me move the boulder, Father?"

The father replied, "Now, my son, you're a man."

I finally sought help in becoming a better dad to my children in 2006. I yearned for a connection with men who could be my friends and confidants, brothers who faced similar joys and sorrows, successes and disappointments, on our path of fatherhood.

I reached out to our pastor, asking him if he'd meet me for coffee during the week between Christmas and New Year's. Despite his busy year-end schedule, he graciously agreed.

"I'd like to meet with a group of men who are in the same stage of life as I am," I told him, "men who are fathers and need other fathers as friends."

"There is no such group," he said. "You'll have to start one, Rich."

So I did.

PART 1

Children Need to Feel *Known*

What does it mean to be **KNOWN**? You know a lot of people, and so do I. But is it possible to know someone without that person *being known* to us? I think it is. It's the difference between being a homeowner and being a tourist who drops into a place, takes in a little of this and a little of that, but never experiences the true essence of the culture.

Megan and I shared two vacations that demonstrate my point. The first vacation was during our pre-kids days, when we went on a Caribbean cruise. We boarded the ship in Miami and sailed to Puerto Rico, where we visited for a day. Then we were off to Saint Thomas and Saint Maarten for a day, and then to Saint John. At each stop, we took group tours, learned a lot of facts about these exotic and beautiful places, and met a few locals who either ran the tours or provided us with food and drink. It was a "been there, done that, got the T-shirt" vacation.

The second vacation was the polar opposite. Megan and I visited County Cork, Ireland, with two-year-old Grace and both of our mothers, to learn more about our family heritage. At first, we did the typical tourist things, like visiting the Waterford crystal plant and some historic castles. Then things changed.

My mother had some distant relatives who lived in County Cork, and we drove down their street. A man stopped us and said in a thick Irish brogue, "You wouldn't happen to be the McMahons would ya?"

"Why, yes! That's us," I answered. My mother's maiden name was McMahon.

"Come this way and park in front of that house there," the man continued, pointing to a quaint brick cottage.

The man, who'd introduced himself as Paddy, led us into his home, where we met my mother's cousin, Deidre, and her great aunt, Gladys. They received us like we were the prodigal family who'd come home after an absence of many years—even though we'd never met.

"You'll stay next door, at my sister's house," Paddy cried out. "She's away on holiday."

"Thank you, Paddy," I answered, "but we have reservations at a bed and breakfast." We didn't want to impose.

"I won't hear of it," he insisted. "What kind of family would we be if we sent you to a hotel?"

We agreed and spent that afternoon and into the wee hours catching up on the lives and dreams of both families. Paddy even managed to get us out to the neighborhood pub for a pint of beer! They offered us heartfelt, extravagant hospitality and shared their lives with us. And we shared our lives with them.

> *To know someone* is to be familiar; *to be known* is to be family.

That is what it means to be known. *To know someone* is to be familiar; *to be known* is to be family.

When I was a tourist in my own life, I was somewhat familiar with my children's interests and activities, and I knew some of their friends but couldn't tell you much about any of them. Now, their friends are like my sons and daughters from another mother. We share stories and experiences, whether it's over a fire pit or watching a movie together. We play games, laugh, and taunt one another. Grace's best friend, whom I've known ten years, interviewed me for a school project. By truly *knowing* my kids' friends, I've made my kids *feel known*.

A tourist is a sightseer. Fathers shouldn't be sightseers. As fathers, we must intentionally invest all of ourselves into all of our children on a continual basis, so they feel known.

CHAPTER 1

◆

I should have started sooner.

After we got married, Megan told me something that forever changed my concept of time and neutralized my fear about being too late. We were on an anniversary date, and we reminisced about how we'd met and retold stories of our dating days. Megan revealed that she'd prayed for me for years before we ever met. I didn't understand.

> As long as you have breath to breathe, and new dreams and fresh prayers, it's never too late to connect with your child and to become the father you were meant to be.

"How can you pray for someone you've never met and aren't sure you'll ever meet?" I asked.

"I trusted that if God meant for me to be married, the right man would enter my life at exactly the right time," she said. "So

I prayed that God would keep you safe and on the right path until it was time for us to find each other."

I was dumbfounded and humbled all at once. What an amazing anniversary gift!

"It's called expectant prayer," she said. "You pray for what you expect God to provide, as it aligns with God's will for your life."

What kind of prayers do you have for your children? What God-size dreams for them do you hold in your heart?

Do you hope they'll graduate high school or college, find a job, and get married to the man or woman of their dreams? Whatever your prayer or dream for your children is, it's not too late for you to be part of it. As long as you have breath to breathe, and new dreams and fresh prayers, it's never too late to connect with your child and to become the father you were meant to be.

I was a little late to the game, but the light bulb finally went off for me when Grace was in high school. I was ready to be the father she needed and that I wanted to be. But I had a sinking, horrible feeling that it was too late. She was already a teenager, and I was behind the curve. I was sick about all the time I'd missed while I was chasing my career instead of helping out in her classroom or coaching her sports teams. I wallowed in grief about the things I hadn't done, and I felt the full force of guilt for not starting sooner. Then it dawned on me that I couldn't let these emotions prevent me from doing the right thing *now*.

Maybe, like me, you can see only the mistakes you've made and can't get past that. If that's the case, the best place for you to start is with forgiveness. I don't mean you should run to your kids to ask their forgiveness, although that may come later. I suggest that you forgive *yourself* first. You can't change the past, but you can give everything you have to be fully present for your kids today and for the rest of your life.

But before you jump in with both feet, you might need to spend time to get to know your children first. They aren't the same kids they were two years ago or even six months ago. So find out who they are *now*. Observe them at different times and with different people. What do you see? Are they confident? Shy? Fearful? Joyful?

How do your kids act around you? Do they initiate conversation with you? How do they respond to your calls and texts, or your invitations to spend time together? When you ask them questions, is it like an interrogation? Or do you ask them open-ended questions that invite their answers and seek their opinions? Read their body language and watch their faces. (This means that you both have to look up from your screens for longer than thirty seconds.) Notice how they react to you.

I used to pick up Grace after school and grill her about her day. I asked how much homework she had and what time she needed to be dropped off or picked up at her various activities. I could see her shrivel in the seat next to me and physically withdraw from the force of my questions. She looked like a trapped animal.

Because I've taken time to get to know Grace, I realize now that she needs some time to herself after a busy day at school. So I give her thirty to forty-five minutes to decompress after school, and then we talk. Instead of an interrogation, it's a pleasant exchange between father and daughter. I also make it a point to pick her up in the evenings after choir because that's when she's in a great mood and likes to talk.

My son Luc is a new teenager, and we've gone on some father–son adventures to connect and get to know each other better.

We once took a road trip from Saint Louis to the East Coast to attend his cousin's graduation. We stopped at rest areas along the way, threw a football, and ate all his favorite foods. After awhile, he opened up and told me the back stories of his favorite songs.

It's been easy for me to get to know Luc because he's a lot like me. But as he gets older, he'll need space, too, and I'll have to let go so he can accept the responsibilities that are appropriate for a maturing teen.

IDEAS TO IMPLEMENT

It's never too late to make your relationship with your kids a top priority. That means your kids and their activities take priority over your Saturday golf game, after-work happy hours, business trips that conflict with the school play, and romantic pursuits, if you're single.

> What you *say* isn't important. What you *do* is the only thing that counts. If you put your kids off, your actions show that they're not your priority.

If your son or daughter asks you to play catch, blow bubbles, or help with homework—or if your child simply asks you a question—here's what you do: drop everything and say, "Yes."

Don't forget that you're a bit late to the game here, and a lot of sand has run through the hourglass. Give your child your *full* attention. What you *say* isn't important. What you *do* is the only thing that counts. If you put your kids off, your actions show that they're not your priority.

Say "yes" now. Spend one-on-one time with each child. Have fun, but make sure you're fully present, so your children can—if they wish—tell you what's on their minds and in their hearts.

Here are some ideas to help you make your children a priority in your life:

1. Create Time for Them—Shift your schedule and carve out time that works best for *them*, when *they're* most receptive. For example, I'm a morning person and Grace is a night owl. So when I tried to talk with her at breakfast and in the car on the way to school, it annoyed her.

Then, one morning as we were driving to school, I quietly prayed for her and for her day, her friends, her teachers, and her activities until I ran out of things to pray about.

"What can I pray for you today, Grace?" I asked her.

"Well," she said, "I have a biology test today. You could pray for that."

Now I ask her this question every so often to give her an opportunity to tell me about her concerns and joys, if she wants to. There's no interrogation, and she doesn't feel like I'm prying where I don't belong.

Because mornings aren't her prime time, we decided to have lunch and coffee dates instead. I even got her to let me take her out to a nice dinner—just the two of us, all dressed up.

To make Luc a priority, I became an assistant coach for his baseball team, and I throw pitches at practice and hit ground balls for the team to field. We travel to and from the ball fields together, and every once in a while, the two of us stop for a bite to eat or an ice cream.

Zoey, our youngest, always has to tag along while Megan or I shuttle the other kids to their activities. So one time, I packed up a softball and our gloves, and we drove to a park while waiting for Luc's practice to be over. I pretended to be the ump and catcher while Zoey fast-pitched in the college world series for the Lady Vols of Tennessee! Zoey and I grew to love this one-on-one time.

2. Do What They Love—Our youth pastor once advised me to "love what they love." Who are your child's favorite singers, authors, and actors? What are their favorite books, movies, and superheroes? If you don't know, ask!

I'd noticed that Grace was reading *Divergent*, which had just been released; on several occasions, I saw her poring over the book, lost in its pages.

"Hey, Grace," I said, "do you like that book?"

"Yeah, it's pretty good," she mumbled. Clearly, I was interrupting, but I continued.

"Do you think I'd like it?"

"You might."

"Can I borrow it when you're finished?"

Grace nodded.

When the movie was released some time later, it hit our city with a midnight premiere. Fully caught up in that fantasy world, Grace made it clear that she had to go. So I took her and a friend to the midnight show—and I'm definitely not a night owl!

The girls dressed up as their favorite characters from the adventurous Dauntless faction. In the book, the Dauntless are exactly what their name implies: dauntless. They never wait for a train to stop before they board or exit; they simply jump on and off speeding trains.

We pulled up to theater, and, in my most dramatic voice, I said, "Get ready, girls. I'll drive by, so you can jump out and prove that you're Dauntless!"

Grace's friend looked straight at me, her face showing her surprise. "Did you read the book, Mr. Daniels?"

"Of course!" I exclaimed.

I was becoming better and better at following the good advice I'd been given: love what they love, and you love them. And I earned some major points that night with both my daughter and her friend.

3. Show You Know Your Child—Show you know your children by making each of them a personalized "favorites" collage or shadow box. I know what you're thinking: "No way! I don't do crafts. I've got no idea where to start." I didn't either, but I figured it out. Remember: love what they love!

I packed up all three kids, and we drove to a nearby Michael's crafts store. When we got inside, they all took off to their favorite area, while I just stood there. I didn't know where to go or what to look for.

An associate approached me and said, "You look like you could use some help. You've got that 'It's my first time in Michael's' look on your face."

"That obvious, huh?"

"It's OK. We get that a lot in here," she replied.

"I want to make a shadow box for my wife and each of my kids. I want to put their favorite things in it," I explained.

"Let's start by finding some great boxes," she recommended, "and you can tell me what they each like."

I picked out an appropriate box for each of them, and we headed down the knick-knack aisle. We passed a lot of things that I'd never seen before, and I had no idea how they could be used. With her help, I filled a small basket with trinkets, stickers, ornaments, and assorted bric-a-brac. For Grace, I selected some musical notes, artistic stickers, and flowers. I got Luc wooden and plastic pieces with images of the sun, smiles, baseballs and bats, and a microphone. For Zoey, I chose stickers with images of a basketball, softball, unicorn, and Lady Vols.

"When you get home," she said, "search YouTube for shadow box videos showing how to assemble it all."

The kids and I went home and sat around the kitchen table while I created Megan's shadow box first and then made one for each of the kids. It was a lot of fun, and they all loved and appreciated their gifts.

You can create shadow boxes for your family, just as I did. It's a great way to capture the essence of your child's dreams and favorite things.

4. Come Alongside Them—Kids have a lot of things to do, and they sometimes may need your help. But they may not know how to ask for help—especially while you're developing your relationship with them. So your job is to look for opportunities either to help your kids or to join them in what they're doing.

If a child seems to be struggling with a regular homework assignment or a special project, offer your assistance and see the activity through until it's finished. On occasion, surprise your children by helping with their chores. For example, empty the dishwasher or fold laundry together; or make dinner as a team and clean up afterward. These are daily tasks of life, and you can make them fun for your children.

When you come alongside your children, you also have an opportunity to get to know them better by creating a conversation that isn't threatening. What's their favorite food, candy, book, subject, author, song, singer, movie, TV show, actor/actress, sports team, player, video game, or breakfast food? It may take awhile for your children to trust your motives, but remember that this relationship thing is new to them, too. It may take some time for you to build their trust.

5. Make a List of Their Dreams—I keep a journal for each of my kids, and I record their dreams in it. Of course, their dreams change every year or even more frequently, so it's an ongoing activity. Here are some questions I asked my children to help you get started:

- What is your dream job? (What do you want to be when you grow up?) Why?

- What is your dream school? Why? (for high school kids who are looking at colleges) What is your dream place— anywhere in the world—to live? Why?

- What is your dream vacation? Why?

- What is your dream house or room? Why?

- What is your dream adventure? Why?

- Who is your dream boyfriend or girlfriend? Why?

The younger your kids are when you start this, the better. But if you're in the waning years of your children's time at home, this may be your last chance to learn about their dreams, ambitions, and hopes for the future. So dive in and do it!

I wanted a way to encourage my two daughters to follow their dreams, so I made a jar I call "A Daughter's Dreams." I searched online for the top twenty-five things that psychologists and other professionals say a girl needs from her father, wrote them on a piece of paper, and dropped them in the jar. As I spent more and more time with Grace and Zoey, and learned more about them, I added to the jar some of my own ideas for making them feel know, valued, and loved—for example, "dance with your daughter before school" and "share a fierce hug."

I told Zoey about some of my ideas, and she started to dance with me. Then, for my birthday one year, she gave me a journal that she had decorated with word stickers reflecting things the two of us loved and shared together. Two of the words were *fierce* and *hugs*. Now, whenever I come home from work or from a trip, Zoey bounds down the stairs or leaps off the couch to give me a fierce hug. I drop my backpack or computer case and brace for the impact—which is so fierce that our dog, Skipper, runs right behind her, ready to pounce!

I did something different to learn about Luc. When he was ten, we went on a father–son day to Six Flags. On the way, we stopped at a coffee shop to grab a bite to eat. I gathered up a bag filled with multicolored flag banners that I'd bought, the kind you see at car lots, along with some markers and stickers, and took it into the coffee shop.

While we waited for our food, I said, "Name some words that describe the character of the kind of man you'd like to be."

"Honest," he suggested.

"Great one," I said. "Write *honest* on the first flag. What's another word?"

"Courageous?" he asked.

"Yes, courageous so you can overcome fears. Write *courageous* on the next flag. Can you think of some other words?"

"Loyal. Patient. Persevering."

"Yes, yes, and yes!" I exclaimed. "What does perseverance mean to you?"

"Not quitting," he answered.

"Spot on!" I said. "Like winners never quit, and quitters never win."

The waitress appeared at our table with our food, and as we munched down our breakfast sandwiches, I asked, "Any other words you can think of, Luc?"

"Integrity?"

"Yes, that's a great one," I said. "Do you know what *integrity* means?"

"It means being honest with yourself, like doing the right thing even when no one else is watching."

"You're amazing, buddy," I replied.

I hadn't taught Luc any of these words, so I asked, "Where'd you learn all this stuff?"

"From the Value Tales I read with Mom before bed," he said.

After he'd written a word on each of the flags, I showed him the stickers of superheroes that I'd bought.

"Let's focus on one or two of these words each week," I said. "I'll ask you to tell me a story about a time when you showed courage, patience, integrity, or another word that's written on a flag. For every story you tell, you'll get to put a sticker on one of the flags."

Luc and I played this private game, which we called "Flags of Our Fathers," for about six months. Luc is fourteen now, and I recently found the flags in his room. Curious about the impact that our game had on him, I asked, "Hey, Luc, what does it take to be a man?"

Without missing a beat, he answered, "Hair."

OK, so I can't guarantee the results. But life is real.

I want my children to become people of character, and the path to character comes by persevering in times of struggle. Without the struggle, there's no perseverance; without perseverance, we never develop character. Of course, I don't want my kids to struggle just for the sake of struggle. The struggles will certainly come, and I pray they'll be able to persevere.

6. Feed Their Dreams—Zoey's dream is to play on the softball team at her mom's alma mater, the University of Tennessee Lady Vols. One Saturday the Lady Vols were playing about ninety minutes from where we lived, so I took Zoey to the game. It was one of those sunny, crisp spring days that was just made for a bat and ball. And we got lucky: we sat right next to the Lady Vols' bullpen.

Zoey's eyes were wild with excitement as she watched the pitchers and catchers warm up. THWAP! The speed of the pitching put her in a frenzy before the game even began. Turning to me, she declared, "I'm going to pitch even faster than that when I play for the Lady Vols!"

"I know you will, Zoey!" I exclaimed. "But I'm not sure I'll still be able to catch for you then."

"That's OK, Dad," she said. "You'll be watching with Mom from the stands, and your faces will be painted orange and white!"

When I heard Zoey talk about her dreams with such clarity and certainty, I almost burst. I'd wanted to give her a special afternoon, but that's what she gave me.

After the game, we waited over an hour for the team to come out of their locker room. Zoey stood in the brisk, late-afternoon breeze, proudly wearing her Lady Vols T-shirt, and said to the first player who came out, "Excuse me. Can we get a picture with you?"

The player looked at Zoey, saw her Lady Vols T-shirt, and knew that Zoey had waited well over an hour for this moment.

"We can do one better," the player said. Turning toward her teammates who were pouring out of the locker room, she shouted, "Hey, girls, we have a future Lady Vol over here, and she wants to get a picture with us."

The entire team came over to take a photo with Zoey. One of the stars, Rainey Gaffin, signed Zoey's shirt and gave her a high five that she'll never forget—the perfect ending to a priceless adventure that Zoey and I will share for a lifetime.

What Is Required of Me?

If you're starting out with a deficit and need to get to a neutral place before you try some of the ideas in this chapter, you might need to seek forgiveness and grace from your child first. Have a short one-on-one moment before your child goes to bed or is in an open mood.

Simply say, "I'm sorry I haven't been the dad that you need and deserve. That's in the past. I'm going to do better, and it starts right now. I may not get it right every time, but I want

> It's never, ever too late to be a good father to your children.

you to know that I love you, and I'm committed to be with you throughout your life as your greatest supporter and biggest fan. Can we start over?"

Remember that love is patient. Be love. Even though you'd like to flip the on switch on the relationship, your child may need some time to believe in the new you. And your child may be suspicious of your motives. That's normal. Just stick with it while you earn your child's trust and form a new relationship.

It's never, ever too late to be a good father to your children. You always have *now*. *Now* write a note to each of your children. *Now* find out about their favorite things and discover their dreams. Call them *now*. Text your children *now*. Ask them to help you create a Snapchat or Instagram account *now*. Ask your children *now* how you can pray for them.

Start *now*.

CHAPTER 2

◆

I don't know how
to communicate with
my children.

I was on a training adventure in the Ardennes region in Belgium—an area of rough terrain, forests, and ridges—and I was the leader of one of four teams. All team members were blindfolded, and we were dropped off deep in the woods in four separate, remote locations. The goal was for the four teams to meet up before it got dark—in about two hours.

Each team was given a different set of tools for navigation. The first team had a walkie-talkie with two-way communication. The second team had half of a map showing only the area where they were dropped off and a walkie-talkie with only one-way communication, so they could listen but not talk.

The third team had half of a map showing an area where they *hadn't been* dropped off—but they didn't know that—as well as a two-way walkie-talkie. The fourth team, my team, had both halves of a map and a two-way walkie-talkie. This was clearly an exercise in effective communication, which we all knew going in.

As soon as my team was dropped off and removed our blindfolds, I used our walkie-talkie to announce that we had two maps and a two-way walkie-talkie. Then I asked the other teams about their resources so we could take a full inventory. Team 1 reported they had no map. Team 2 remained silent, so we concluded that they could only listen. Team 3 said they had half a map.

I asked each team to look around and orient themselves on their maps, while our team did the same. Before we could do anything else, we had to figure out each team's starting location. Once we determined that, my team identified a central meeting location that could be easily located and identified by every team.

Then I issued instructions to the other three teams. I told Team 1 to follow the pine tree line and head toward the river. I instructed Team 2 to follow the river upstream to the meeting point, which was only an hour away from them. With a one-way walkie-talkie, Team 2 couldn't confirm the instruction, so we had to trust that they'd heard and understood. Team 3, which was in the middle of the woods, an hour due south of the meeting point, had a West Point grad as a team member; I assumed they could discern north from south, so I instructed them to head due north until they reached the river. My team, Team 4, headed down the trail toward the meeting point, feeling confident that we'd make it within an hour.

Thirty minutes later, I checked in with the other three teams to see how they were doing.

"Team 1, this is Team 4," I said. "Have you reached the river yet?"

"Team 4, this is Team 1. Yes, we've reached the river." Team 1 was on track.

"Team 1, this is Team 4," I continued. "Follow the river downstream until you meet up with Team 2."

"Team 4, this is Team 1. Roger that. Heading downstream to meet up with Team 2."

Team 2 had no way to communicate with us, but they could hear us. So I said, "Team 2, this is Team 4. Continue to follow the river upstream until you run into Team 1. You should pass a big boulder on the right and an old hunting lodge on the ridge to the left."

We didn't know if they were headed in the right direction, but we trusted that they could hear us and continued to reassure them.

Team 3 checked in, and I said, "Team 3, this is Team 4. Describe what you see around you."

"Team 4, this is Team 3. We're crossing a large field, and the mountains are on our left."

Our map showed that Team 3 should have been in thick woods, with the mountains on their right. Instead of heading due north, Team 3 had headed due south. We were able to get them turned around, but we estimated that it would now take them ninety more minutes to reach the meeting point, so we probably wouldn't meet our objective. As it turned out, three teams found the meeting place on time, but Team 3 arrived thirty minutes late.

I related this story because it reveals the approach we followed, which you can use to communicate with your children:

1. **Listen**—We listened to each other to take inventory and determine our respective starting points.

2. **Be a Team**—We were four groups with a shared objective, acting as a cohesive team.

3. **Find a Way In**—We made adjustments to help one group get back on track and find the way.

LISTEN

Think about the last few conversations you had with your child. Were you the one who talked the most, or did you listen to him or her? Did you try to understand your child, or did you press your point, so your child would understand you?

When Luc was about thirteen, I picked him up after dance lessons, and he told me he didn't want to go anymore. Luc loved to sing, act, and perform, and dance had always been a part of that. It seemed natural to me that, at thirteen, he wouldn't want to do it anymore. But I knew something that he didn't: quitting could limit his opportunities for future stage performances at school.

"Why do you want to quit?" I asked.

"I just don't want to do it anymore," he said.

"What changed?" I asked.

After several seconds of silence, he told me, "I'm the only boy in the class, and I get singled out a lot."

"What do you mean by 'singled out'?" I asked.

"You know, the teacher singles me out to teach me a new step in front of the whole class," he explained. "Everyone stares at me. It's embarrassing. I don't like being the only one."

Luc's story brought to mind an experience I'd had when I was about his age. I wasn't going to try out for the next level of baseball because, if I were selected, I wouldn't be playing ball with my friends anymore. But my parents made me go to the tryouts. If they hadn't forced me to go, I never would have experienced a great year of baseball or won a championship. Although I was the only one of my group of friends who was on the team, I was doing what I loved.

I told Luc the story and then said, "That championship year was the same year I broke my jaw, and all my teammates signed the game ball and gave it to me. I still have that baseball. If I'd let my fears stop me, I would have missed the chance to improve my skills, as well as some pretty amazing experiences.

"I'm not trying to preach to you, Luc. I'm simply sharing something I learned at your age. As your dad, I could let you quit and possibly regret it later, or I could make you go, even though you'd probably resent my making you do it. So it's your choice."

> My role was to help Luc sort the facts from the fear of what others might think, as he continued toward his dreams, desires, and goals.

My role was to help Luc sort the facts from the fear of what others might think, as he continued toward his dreams, desires, and goals.

The next week, he was upset again and didn't want to go to class. Tears welled in his eyes, and he shrunk in the seat next to me.

"Why don't you go in and learn one new dance step?" I suggested. "It's important not to let what other people think—or might think—keep you from pursuing your goals. The sooner you learn that someone else's thoughts, words, and actions can't dictate your own thoughts, words, and actions, the closer you'll be to achieving your dreams and goals."

He didn't budge.

"If you still decide you don't want to dance," I said, "I'll respect your decision. I just want it to be your decision for your own reasons."

It's important to observe *what* your child says and *how* he says it. Luc still loved music and dance, and he wanted to ultimately be an actor. He had a natural ability and was gifted in dance. But after that class, he decided to drop dance lessons after six years of instruction. I listened and respected his decision.

BE A TEAM

> It's a lot easier to communicate with your kids if they know you're on their side.

It's a lot easier to communicate with your kids if they know you're on their side. If you don't listen to them, or if you jump down their throats for the slightest infraction or failure, they'll never open up to you and trust you. And who could blame them?

When your family is a team, each member feels like he belongs. A good coach knows the talents and shortcomings of each player and makes sure that players play to their strengths. Like a good coach, you have to know your children first.

For fun, our family formed the Bean Team. I'd earned the nickname "Bean" when I jumped out of bed from a dead sleep one night after a loud thunderclap broke over our house. My wife said I looked like a Mexican jumping bean, and the name had stuck.

So the Bean Team came out in force to cheer me on the first time I ran a marathon. We each had a special name and a role to fill. Megan was Coffee Bean because she was in charge of coffee and donuts. Grace, who was Jelly Bean, made beautiful signs to encourage me along the route. Luc was String Bean, and his job was to run up and get in the front row to cheer me on. Zoey, with her outdoor, rugged nature, was Baked Bean, and she yelled the loudest. I, of course, was Daddy Bean.

The Bean Team name was now ours, and we adopted the practice of doing a team cheer before and after other races and at the kids' events.

"Bean Team on three," one of us would yell. "One, two, three—Bean Team!"

Good leaders provide guidance. As the leader of your team, you can help your kids set goals and give them support as they pursue them. But beware. There's a fine line between supporting your kids and doing too much for them. Remember that the results are always up to the child.

> There's a fine line between supporting your kids and doing too much for them. Remember that the results are always up to the child.

For example, every season Luc picks a specific area in his sport that he wants to improve. One year he wanted to hit better, so I arranged for him to take hitting lessons, and I drove him to the batting cages so he could practice. As a result, his performance on the field improved.

Zoey wanted to learn how to pitch in fast-pitch softball, and we found someone to teach her. Her lessons taught her the proper technique, and her pitching accuracy and speed improved dramatically.

Grace loves to sing, and Megan and I support her in this passion. Whether she goes to choir practice, takes voice lessons, or stretches herself in a vocal jazz group at school, Grace sets her own goals and achieves them.

When Grace was in eighth grade, she wanted to try out for her first school musical. When she learned the musical would be *My Fair Lady,* she watched the movie and religiously practiced all the songs on her own. Grace's determination and preparation earned her the lead role.

> As the leader of your team, it's even more important to join your children when they fall short.

But what about when your child fails? As the leader of your team, it's even more important to join your children when they fall short and to help them figure out how to succeed the next time.

One year, Luc's goal was to win both the design award and the speed award at the Boy Scouts Pinewood Derby Race. Luc is very creative, and he made a really cool iPod car—and it was fast! But he won only the design award and left the event with disappointment written all over his face.

"Why are you disappointed, Luc? You won the design award," I said.

"I wanted to win the design award *and* the speed award," he replied.

"So what do you think you need to do next year to win both awards?"

"I need to pick a design that distributes the weight like the fastest cars," Luc explained with certainty.

"Right on, buddy!"

Zoey encountered failure at her first science fair. Together, we'd worked long and hard to build a liquid lava lamp. She had her heart set on the blue ribbon, but she got only a participant award. As difficult as it was for her, we reviewed the scoring sheet together to learn what she'd missed and how she could do a better job the next time. After our conversation, she understood that she'd have to follow the very specific instructions to the letter to earn a blue ribbon at the next science fair.

Instead of joining with my children, if I'd blamed them for their shortcomings, they'd have felt rejection, and our communication would have been damaged—possibly for years. It takes a long time for a child to recover from those kinds of parental wounds. But when we come alongside our children and help them process their disappointment, we prove that we're on their team and that we support them. When we care about their feelings and feel what they feel, they feel known.

Find a Way In

If connecting with your children has been difficult in the past or is new to you, you need to find a way in. Why not invite your kids in with a story?

You might, for example, tell them a story about something that you're struggling with. Be specific, and tell them precisely what troubles you. Be vulnerable about your challenges, your fears, and your failures, and don't be afraid to say that you've made some good decisions as well as some bad ones that taught you valuable lessons. Ask for their help, and then show that you value their ideas and opinions.

I was a partner in a start-up company, YurBuds, that made sport headphones. We had a big project to build our brand identity and had to pick the "face" of our company from an array of photographs. I brought all the images home and spread them out on the living room floor. Grace came in from choir, and I asked her which photo would best represent our brand. She had a keen eye for art and detail, and I explained that we wanted to do more than sell sport headphones. We wanted to inspire and motivate people to live active, healthy lives.

Grace looked at all the faces, then pointed to one.

"That one," she said.

"Abby?" I asked. "Why did you choose her?"

"It's her eyes," Grace said. "A determination comes through her eyes."

As it turned out, we did choose Abby as the face of our brand, and she became an icon at retail outlets, on social media, and at promotional events. We created a shirt on which her face and the brand logo appeared along with the message, "Don't wait for inspiration to find you. Become it." The shirt became iconic.

When I came home with the shirts bearing Abby's face, Grace exclaimed, "That's the one I picked!"

"Yep," I said. "We agreed this was the best one. We liked Abby, too."

Grace felt affirmed that I valued her opinion, and for quite awhile she would go for runs wearing the "Abby shirt" and a big smile on her face.

But it doesn't have to be something big like branding your company for you to ask for your child's opinion. For example, enlist a child's help in simple, daily choices: "What do you think about this tie?" or "Should I wear the red tie or the blue one?" Every Christmas, Zoey gets to choose the tie I wear—either my Grinch tie or my Christmas tree tie. I wouldn't have it any other way.

Speaking of ties, one year Grace made me a duct-tape tie that I wore to church. Her friend, the pastor's daughter, had made a tie for her dad as well. When the pastor—who was proud of his daughter's handiwork, said, "I bet no one else has a tie like this one," Grace nudged me to stand up and show off my tie. Of course, I stood with great fanfare, and Grace was thrilled.

IDEAS TO IMPLEMENT

There are doubtlessly lots of types of stories that would capture your kids' attention and imagination and get a conversation going. Even a news story can spark their interest. Of course, when you plant a seed and you wait for it to grow, sometimes all you see is the fertilizer! But if you're persistent and try different approaches, you'll learn how to communicate with your kids. And when you listen to them and show that you understand their feelings, they'll know that you truly know and love them.

Here are some things to try:

- Explore new places to find stories and interesting topics to discuss.

- Start with something light and fun, and build authentic stories together.

- Listen to the latest TED talk on National Public Radio, and discuss it with your kids.

- Check out Gabe Lyons at Q Ideas (qideas.org), a good source of topics and stories. Go beyond the hype of the media and seek topics and stories that allow you to go deeper and open up to your kids in both heart and mind.

- Initiate a conversation with your children about how you can do a better job of communicating with them. Find a time for this discussion when they're in a particularly good mood, for example, after a fun event or when you're out for ice cream. Tell your kids that you want to communicate with them in ways that they appreciate, and ask them what that looks like.

What Is Required of Me?

To be a better communicator, you must be an *intentional* listener and an *open-ended* questioner. Be a bit of a Sherlock Holmes: observe your kids and figure out when it's best to have conversations with them. Find each of your children's prime time and make those times your prime time together.

Where you communicate is also important. Create space where you and your children feel at ease to talk, where you can share news of the day and joys and concerns of their hearts.

CHAPTER 3

◆

My kids won't listen to me.

One summer, Luc's team was playing in a baseball tournament. He always listened to his coaches and followed their instructions, while I cheered from the stands and loudly hollered, "Load early, buddy."

Luc would shake his head as my advice landed on his ears, clearly unhappy with my unsolicited input. I was out of bounds. His coaches were the ones who instructed him. I only added pressure, and Luc didn't like it one bit.

The situation was entirely different, however, when I filled in as assistant coach. Luc listened and responded to my instruction because I was in an official role and had the authority to help him and his teammates—not the dad in the stands who shouted at his son to perform better.

The lesson here is that fathers must learn when to step back and let others influence, teach, and coach their kids.

Maybe you're like me. I often feel that my kids don't listen to me and won't take my instruction. Nothing riles me like that.

> Sometimes we need to learn when to step back and let others influence them, teach them, and coach them.

"Hey, Luc," I shouted up the stairs. "Meet me outside, please. I want to show you something." I walked out the garage and rolled the lawnmower toward Luc.

"Luc, I think you're ready to use the lawnmower. I was thirteen when I started mowing the lawn, and even though you're still twelve, I think you're ready for this."

"Really? That would be awesome."

We had a small, flat lawn, so the size of the task was perfect for his first opportunity to use the lawnmower.

"Let's start by filling the gas tank and checking the oil," I said. "I'll show you how and you can do it. OK?"

"OK!" he replied.

Luc tightened the cap on the oil reservoir, turned to me, and, with immense satisfaction, said, "Done!"

"Great job, buddy. After we start the mower, you'll cut in an overlapping pattern and mow the entire lawn—like this."

I pushed the mower up one lane and down the next to show him how to overlap the tire tracks in the grass.

"Never reach under the mower," I cautioned. "And don't come up beside it when it's turned on. You could get a permanent injury that way. Understand?"

"Got it," Luc confirmed.

"Ready?" I asked.

"Ready! Let's do this!" Luc declared.

I sat on the front porch and watched Luc carefully cut the grass in the pattern I'd showed him, feeling a slight bit of satisfaction that I'd transferred some knowledge to my son. He was following my instructions—carefully and enthusiastically—and I forgot about all the times I'd felt that he hadn't listen to me.

After a few rows, Luc got the hang of it. But when I asked him to recut a couple of gaps in the middle of the yard, he got mad and wanted to quit.

"It takes a few times to get good at something," I explained, "and it takes a lot of practice to get great at anything."

Luc didn't want to practice; he wanted to be great right from the start. So much for my fleeting sense of satisfaction.

"It's just like in baseball, buddy," I told him. "You know how your pitching coach helped you learn the proper technique? You listened to what he said, made a few throws, got some feedback, and then threw a few more using a better technique. After you practiced a bit, you threw a great two-seam fastball."

Of course, I told that story to remind Luc of a time when he had to practice something difficult before he got much better at it. But my words fell on deaf ears. Luc stormed off into the house.

Two years later, when Luc was fourteen, I broached the subject of responsibility with Luc at a father–son dinner.

"Part of growing up is having more responsibility," I said. "Do you know what responsibility is?"

"It's taking care of things you need to do," Luc replied.

"Exactly," I confirmed. "And as you're given more and more responsibility, you don't want to view it as a punishment or have a bad attitude about it. Try to think about responsibility as having the freedom and power to be in control of your own choices. When you do what you *need* to do before you do what you *want* to do, it shows that you're responsible. And then, it causes Mom and me to trust you more and to give you more freedoms. Do you understand?"

Luc nodded.

Although I'm not always certain how well my kids are listening to me—it's easy for a kid to nod after his dad has told him something—it's still my responsibility to talk about lessons that are important for my children to learn. I trust that, in time, some of what I've said will help Luc, Grace, and Zoey make the right choices for themselves. I've even started to write down some life lessons and have given these letters to my children as keepsakes. Maybe these letters will come in handy after I'm gone or when my children are raising their own children.

When you spend focused time with your kids and talk to them about what's important to you, you help your children feel known. And, hopefully, they'll remember what you said when they start making decisions on their own.

Language Matters

You've heard it before: It's not just *what* you say, it's *how* you say it. But have you ever really listened to yourself?

Maybe you're bossy and bark orders, like I did to Luc from the bleachers. Or maybe your questions are actually thinly veiled accusations that put your child on the defensive. Do you "should" all over your kids?

It's taken me awhile, but I've learned not to say things like, "I think you *ought* to …." It's much more effective, I've found, to ask my kids questions that lead them to think things through for themselves.

Your family is a team, remember? They have to know that you're on their side. So you might say something like, "How could you respond in such a situation next time?" or "How could you approach that situation differently next time?" Not only does this approach improve our communications, it also helps our children learn important thinking and problem-solving skills that will serve them well throughout their lives.

This takes practice, and it's not what I learned as a child. As one of five kids in a devout Catholic home, I was taught to always respect people in authority—adults, teachers, policemen, clergy, elected officials. You get it. But today's children have learned that people in authority aren't always trustworthy—and for good reason. Adults and parents can no longer force their will on children. We must earn their *respect* if we want their *cooperation*.

I'll never forget when Luc got interested in wrestling, four or five years after some of the other kids had taken up the sport. Luc did his best to catch up—he went to all the practices, worked hard, and tried to learn all the moves. He knew five or six of them but hadn't mastered any. After observing him at an especially tough practice, I asked, "What could you do this week to improve your skills, Luc, so you score more points in the next match?"

"I could pick one move, master it, and use it in the match," he replied.

"OK," I said. "Which move?"

"The single-leg lift," he replied.

In doing the single-leg lift, the wrestler dives down, grabs one of his opponent's legs, and lifts it as high as he can, causing the opponent to fall. Then the wrestler jumps on top of his opponent, scoring two points for a takedown.

"Great! You can practice on me at home all week and give it your best shot in Saturday's match," I said.

I went with Luc to all of his practices that week, so I'd know how his coaches taught the move. At home, when Luc was finally able to take me down—at six feet, one hundred ninety pounds—we both knew he was ready for the match.

Luc's first opponent was also a first-year wrestler. When the ref blew the whistle, Luc went after the boy's leg, lifted it up, and took the boy down. He was so proud of himself that, instead of jumping on top of the boy for the two-point take-down, he turned to me and raised his arms in triumph. The match ended up going into extra time, and I reminded Luc that to win, he had to score first. When the whistle sounded again, Luc executed his single-leg lift and takedown perfectly—and he got his first win.

Luc and I exchanged a look that said we both knew how hard he'd worked over the past week to get this win. That's what being known looks like. No words were needed.

When I asked Luc to think about what he could do to win and which move he wanted to master, I gave him a *voice* and a *choice*—which made him feel known and valued. He got to work out his own problem, and I supported him in achieving a goal that was important to him.

I had a similar experience with Zoey when she started to play basketball in the first grade. She was frustrated because she thought that she didn't get the ball enough.

"Do you want to learn the secret of winning in basketball?" I asked.

Of course, she said, "Yes!"

"All basketball games are won by the team that scores the most points, and the secret to having the most points is scoring the most baskets. To score the most baskets, you need to have the ball more than the other team—more possessions," I explained. "Do you understand, Zoey?"

"I do," she confirmed.

"How can you increase your number of possessions?" I asked.

"We can steal the ball away," she said.

"True, but the rules for first graders say that you can't steal the ball. Stealing isn't allowed until you get to the next level. But there's another really big way to get the ball more often."

"How?" she asked.

"You can grab the ball for a rebound after they miss a shot. And you can do that on both ends of the court. That's the big secret!" I said.

"Do you want to learn how to become the top rebounder— to get the most possessions and the most shots?" I asked.

"Yes!" she shouted.

I taught my future Lady Vol how to position herself for the rebound and how to keep her opponent away without fouling her. Zoey practiced the move all the time. During that basketball season, very few first graders crashed the boards to get rebounds, but Zoey was voracious in the next game. She got a rebound under her team's basket, shot it back up, and made her first basket from an offensive rebound. She looked over at me with that knowing look. Priceless!

During the next several basketball games, Zoey continued her rebound craze. She could also dribble the entire length of the floor and then shoot the ball. Her next lesson was how to pass to her teammates!

When your children experience the thrill of success after following your instruction, they become so much more willing to listen to you about other things. When they know their success is an outcome of your instruction, you confirm that you know them—deeply. Celebrate those moments.

It's more effective, of course, to ask your kids how and when they want your help. Don't force yourself on them. Respect them as individuals, and learn who they are and how to engage with them.

Listen First

> You're their father, and they don't forget it when you shoo them away; it hurts them—way down deep. That's what rejection looks like.

If we want our children to be better listeners, we have to show them what listening looks like. I realized that if my kids asked me a question while I was on my computer or watching a football game, I modeled the exact *opposite* of good listening. In fact, I didn't even *try* to listen. I'd grunt at them with that half-attention that's actually a brush off. Now, I try very hard to give them my full attention and answer their question—no matter what I'm doing.

Sound impossible? Unreasonable? If you come from the "children should be seen and not heard" school, this will be tough for you. But isn't that attitude kind of selfish? Children are a bundle of needs, and they look to you, as their dad, to fulfill their needs.

Sure, children talk a lot and interrupt, and it often isn't convenient to drop everything to pay attention to them. But you're their father, and they don't forget it when you shoo them away; it hurts them—way down deep. That's what rejection looks like. And every time that happens, another little piece of their confidence, self-esteem, and sense of self-worth dies.

Of course, you could set boundaries in advance and ask your kids to let you enjoy the game in peace. But wouldn't it be better if you invited them to enjoy the game with you?

Something else I've discovered is that when I want to teach my kids something that they're struggling to do, it's far better to ask some leading questions and listen to their answers first. After I do that, they're usually in the right frame of mind to receive my pointers.

The first time we put up our new ping-pong table, Luc dove right in to play, but he got frustrated whenever he missed a point.

"Why are you getting mad?" I asked.

"Because I'm losing all the time," he snapped.

"Let me ask you something, Luc. What is your goal during each point?" I inquired.

"To get the ball back over the net," he replied.

"Anywhere over the net?" I continued.

"Yeah," Luc muttered.

"My goal is different. I want to return the ball to an area that's either hard for you to reach or that forces you to use your forehand, which I've noticed is weaker than your backhand," I explained. "Which is my weaker shot?" I asked.

"Forehand," Luc said.

"Yes, so try to hit the ball to my forehand or somewhere that makes it hard for me to return it. Want to play another game to try it?"

"Sure," he said.

Luc, who has great hand-eye coordination, acted on that tip and saw that I missed more balls and that his score went up. As simple as my tip was, I made a point to listen to what Luc was trying to accomplish before I made my suggestions.

LISTEN AS A LIFELINE

Late one night, I was away on business in my hotel room, when my phone pinged. It was a text message from Grace, my sixteen-year-old.

> Can I call U? I really need to talk.

Grace had never sent me a text like this. What did she want to talk about at eleven thirty at night? Her depression? Anxiety? School? Mom? Friends? College?

> Sure.

I texted her back:

The phone rang immediately. Grace was crying.

"Why are you so upset, honey?" I asked.

"I haven't been doing my school assignments and turning them in like I told you and Mom," Grace explained between sobs.

"What's going on, Grace? Is there something you want to tell me?" I was pretty sure that there had to be more than missing assignments to make her so upset.

"My depression has been really bad the past few weeks, and I was afraid to tell you guys about my homework," she confessed.

"I'm so glad you called. This weekend, we'll talk about what you can do to feel better and how Mom and I can help. OK?"

"Sure," Grace said.

"Why don't we look at what you can do tonight and tomorrow before I get home? Can you put Mom on the phone, so we can let her know what's going on and make sure you're safe?"

"She's asleep, and I don't want to wake her up," Grace protested.

"It's OK, Grace. Mom will understand. You need to be with someone," I told her.

"OK," she answered, sending waves of relief through me. I was grateful that Grace had the courage to ask for help and was willing to be vulnerable enough to share her problems with us so Megan and I could help her find the right solution.

My heart often leans toward tough love, but, thank goodness, I knew this wasn't the time. This was a time to simply listen—to listen to my teenage daughter's confession and to love her through it.

Sometimes simply listening and being with your children is all they need. I've often made the mistake of giving advice or instructing my kids, of using their pain as a teachable moment. How unfair! How can they feel like I'm on their side when I tell them what they *should* have done. That's like rubbing salt in a wound.

> I've often made the mistake of giving advice or instructing my kids, of using their pain as a teachable moment. How unfair!

When I recently went upstairs to say goodnight to Grace and see how her homework was going, I found her on the phone. We'd explicitly asked her not to use the phone after ten o'clock in the evening, so I asked her to hang up and get back to her homework.

"Steve and I just broke up," she said, her eyes filled with tears.

I knew Grace was in pain, but all I could think about was that she wasn't supposed to be on the phone this late at night.

"I'm sorry to hear that," I said, "but you need to get off your phone and back to your homework."

Later, as I prepared for bed and finished packing for my trip the next morning, I couldn't stop thinking about how poorly I'd listened to Grace and how callous my response was. This was a time of need, not correction.

I walked upstairs, gently woke Grace, and apologized for being so insensitive about her breakup. Grace reached out her hand to me, gave my hand a squeeze, and forgave me. When I don't truly listen and respond in an appropriate manner, I must ask my children for forgiveness.

I used to think that listening was a passive act and that—while my mind was occupied with other things—I could get by with nodding my head and saying "mmm hmm" at the appropriate points. That's not listening. That's *pretending* to listen.

Real listening is active. Active listeners make eye contact and repeat what they heard to confirm that they understand. Real listening requires your full attention—and don't think that your kids don't know the difference.

I'm an extrovert, and I often speak before I listen and think while I'm talking. It's a struggle, but I try to discipline myself to listen first and ask questions, so I fully understand what's going on before I respond. Sometimes this is more painful for me than training for an Ironman!

One morning, I was in the car on my way to begin my fourth week in a new job, when Megan called.

"Grace refuses to go to school today," she said. "She's so upset about making a mistake on an assignment that she's crying and won't get out of bed."

Arriving late at work wouldn't look good, but something told me that I needed to be at home with my wife and daughter. When I got back to the house, Grace was still in bed, sobbing. I knew she'd been up late the night before, and I thought her lack of sleep might be a big part of this issue.

I started to console her, accepting her in the state she was in, and telling her that it was going to be OK. I wanted to make her feel safe and loved, so she'd open up and tell me what had happened.

When she finally calmed down enough to speak, I asked her what was wrong.

"I drew a picture for an assignment for the school paper," she said, "and posted it on the group chat without first sending it to the editor. And it was past the deadline. We're *never* supposed to miss a deadline for the newspaper.

"I texted my editor to apologize, but he's going to be mad at me—and he might kick me off the newspaper," she cried.

"What would you do if you were the editor and another student did the same thing?" I asked. "Would you kick the student off? Forgive her? Make this a teachable moment?

"Tell me more about your editor," I asked. "What's he like, and how did he respond?"

"Here's his text," Grace said as she read it out loud:

It's OK. You missed the deadline though, and all posts need to be sent to editors first. The art is good. The topic was more about social issues. My bad for not making this clear.

"Grace, that's a very mature and appropriate response. Here's how I see it. He forgave you from the start. He said, 'It's OK.'

"Then he told you what you need to correct for future assignments: meet the deadline and send to the editor first. And he praised your artwork: 'The art is good.'

"Finally, he shared ownership of the problem: 'My bad for not making this clear.'

"Would you fire someone for doing what you did?" I asked again.

"No," she replied.

"Grace, I think your editor wants to work through this and that you need to muster up the courage and go to school to resolve this. Can you do that?" I asked. "I'll wait for you for twenty minutes and take you to school if you get ready quickly."

With that, Grace's crisis was solved, and she got out of bed and moved forward.

RESPOND VS. REACT

I had to give myself some points for how I'd handled that situation because it could have gone another way. I could have stormed into Grace's room and insisted that she get out of bed and go to school, tough-loving her to get her to do something she clearly didn't want to do. And for me, it wouldn't have been totally out of character.

> When your children are crying out, to love and know them simply means to be there, to be present, to be available.

In my crazy busy, stressed-out, overscheduled world, I frequently react—and overreact—to situations, instead of responding to my kids. When I react without thinking, it looks like anger. I raise my voice, shout, yell, criticize, and even call my children names. When I correct or instruct my kids, what they hear me say is, "I'm right and you're wrong." Their defenses go up, and all communication is shut down. Oh, how I regret that!

In sharp contrast, a thoughtful, appropriate response is punctuated with timely words or actions. I pause, use a gentle tone of voice, assure my child that "accidents happen," and that I've done the same thing before. I forgive my child and say it's OK.

So my message to you is, try to lead your children with love, understanding, kindness and grace, mercy and forgiveness. When your children are crying out, to love and know them simply means to be there, to be present, to be available. Respond rather than react.

To avoid saying something that will damage my kids, I've learned to count to ten or to say a funny word to halt my knee-jerk reactions. This gives me the time I need to come up with a better response. Zoey thinks it's hilarious when I say a crazy word in an expletive moment.

A few years ago, Grace broke a special bowl that Luc had made for me. He had hand-painted my college logo on it, and it was one of my favorite treasures. When Grace accidentally broke it, I shouted, "Rumpelstiltskin!" My silly outburst got everyone laughing, and, while it was important for Luc to hear Grace say that she was sorry for breaking the bowl, we were all able to forgive and move forward.

IDEAS TO IMPLEMENT

- Think about someone your child respects or listens to. What do you observe about that person and their relationship with your child? What does this person say or do differently from you that causes your son or daughter to listen to them? Try to adopt the words and attitudes of this person in your own way of relating to your child.

- When your kids ask for help, they're in a very vulnerable position. Create a positive climate where they feel safe to express this vulnerability. As you build these positive experiences, your children will become more open to your input.

- As a way of getting to know your children better, keep a journal of what you see them do and say, and the feelings they express in various situations.

  - How do they respond when you *react* to them if they do something wrong? Do they open up or shut down? How is their response different when you *respond* to them?

  - Are your kids afraid to do something wrong because of how you'll react?

  - Are they afraid to try new things?

  - Do they fear failure?

  - Are they afraid they won't get your approval and affirmation?

  - Do they try new things and new approaches to solve problems, or do they keep making the same mistakes?

- Try something new together. I remember when I tried to pitch a curveball for the first time; even holding the ball was a challenge. Luc and I watched YouTube videos of curveball grips and pitch techniques, and then we tried the techniques ourselves. It was fun.

- I've often watched Khan Academy videos with Grace to refresh my mind on a particular topic in algebra. And once I went "old school" with Zoey, who is a fierce competitor, and we made a game out of how fast she could shout out the answers as I held up multiplication flash cards.

What Is Required of Me?

First and foremost, you have to become more aware of what you say and do, and the impact on your kids. Moving from knee-jerk reactions to loving responses takes practice. You can make a good start by assessing your last few encounters with your kids and reflecting on how you could be more loving the next time.

If you handle a situation poorly, be vulnerable and ask for your child's forgiveness. Take it a step further and ask your children what you could do to respond better to them.

Finally, develop courageous patience. Have the courage to simply be present when that's all that's needed. Trust that your full presence will help your child feel safe and loved enough to come to you in times of need.

In most cases, your kids want you to model the same thing toward

> Have the courage to simply be present when that's all that's needed.

them that you want for yourself: respect, love, and concern. Actively listen to your kids. Confirm that you understand them by asking deeper questions. Restate what you heard them say to confirm that you heard and understood them. Resist the temptation to give advice or launch into a sermon. Not every moment is a teachable moment.

To create better listeners, create more listening moments when you turn away from what you're doing and give your full attention to your child. Turn off your phone—or, better yet, leave it behind. These opportunities will likely come at the most inopportune times, and they'll force you to make major shifts in your schedule. You can either choose to get angry or accept it as a part of life. Seize these moments as opportunities to make your child feel safe, loved, valued, and known.

Above all, listen first.

CHAPTER 4

◆

Girls—I just don't relate to them.

Let's face it. Daughters are girls, and there's a strong temptation to let their mothers be the go-to parent, especially after they reach a certain age. Boys are easier to relate to. Just throw them a ball, get them in the great outdoors, or play video games with them, and you're in. Girls are more complicated. A girl can be more emotional and sensitive, especially when dealing with a father who doesn't "get" her. But girls can also be deeper thinkers and draw deeper meaning from something, both good and bad, that their father says or does. By the time they reach puberty, their emotions can blow off the scale. Just because you can't relate to *that* doesn't mean you can't relate to *her*.

Your relationships with your daughters can be incredibly special. So my advice to you is to resist the temptation to let her mom be the exclusive go-to parent for your daughters. You'll miss so much if you do.

But what can we fathers do to promote relationships with our daughters? It took me years to have this epiphany, but I finally realized if I learned to love what my daughters love, I could relate to them. So figure out what each of your girls love, and then go out of your way to create experiences around that. When you share in what your daughters love, they feel that you know them. It's that simple.

Love What They Love

We had a tight budget one year and had to forego a full-blown family vacation. Instead, I took a week off and used that time for a one-on-one date day with each of the kids and with Megan.

I wanted to have a great time with each of them and to come away with some shared, memorable experiences. But first, I had to figure out what each of them loved so I could plan an adventure around that.

Grace's adventure began when I extended an invitation to her the day before.

"Hey, Gracie! Be ready at nine o'clock tomorrow morning, and bring your camera. I have a special day planned for us," I said.

Waking up early isn't easy for Grace, but she knew I was taking her to a new, cool coffee house where we'd enjoy fresh crepes and coffee. So she was in the car right on time.

After we'd enjoyed a delicious breakfast, I told Grace, "Here's what I'm thinking. We'll tour the city and take photos at the top ten most photographic churches in Saint Louis."

"Where are they?" she asked with a smile.

"Here's the map," I said. "Let's circle the ones we want to see and figure out the best route to cover them all."

We saw some beautiful small churches tucked away in charming, older neighborhoods before we stopped at the stunning Cathedral Basilica of Saint Louis. Grace looked up and around to soak it all in.

"It's beautiful," she said. "I love the mosaic tiles and stained glass."

As we walked toward the magnificent altar and sanctuary, a visiting choir broke into song. Rich baritones, clear tenors, and lilting soprano voices washed over us, and we basked in the private concert with the perfect acoustics of the marvelous cathedral.

"They sound like angels," Grace whispered. "I've never heard anything so beautiful."

When the choir finished, we walked out the front entrance and headed toward our car. A homeless man was sitting a few feet from where we'd parked, and I decided to stop. In my crazy-busy life, I often see people like this, and I rush right by them after putting a little money in their cups. This time, something told me to stop.

"Good morning," I said.

"Good morning to you," came the reply.

"What's your name?" I asked.

"My name is David."

"Hi, David. I'm Rich, and this is my daughter, Grace. Do you mind if we sit down and visit with you for a minute?" I asked.

"Sure. Nice to meet you. Beautiful day today," he said.

David told us about himself and how he loved the Cathedral Basilica.

"Here," Grace said to David. She dug in her purse and pulled out a few dollars. "Why don't you buy some lunch with this?"

"Well, thank you, Grace," David said.

"Would it be OK if we prayed together?" I asked. "I'd like to thank God for this day and this moment of friendship."

David liked the idea, and we bowed our heads.

I'd been practicing how to be fully present with my kids, but this was the first time I'd been this present with a stranger. And sharing this experience with Grace knit us together in a way we'd never forget.

As we drove to the next church, we talked about our meeting with David and about homelessness.

"I'm normally nervous walking by homeless people," Grace said, "but David was really nice."

"Right," I said. "They're people, just like us. I so often see the *needs* of the needy, but I miss the actual *person*. It was wonderful to meet David and to be present in such a personal way."

This was one of the first times that I'd had a deep and meaningful conversation with Grace as a young adult, rather than as my little girl. I used to miss that little girl and lament the loss, instead of being present with this beautiful soul and looking forward to new experiences at a whole new level. Talking with her as a young adult has helped me relate with her as she grows into her mature self.

I feel very fortunate to have another little girl, Zoey, who is filled with imagination and wonder. When Zoey was eight, Megan and I decided to buy a food truck for our Mexican restaurant, Amigos. I did some online research and found one that looked like it would work for us. However, it was in Kansas City, Kansas—four hours from Saint Louis, across the state line from Kansas City, Missouri. After the owner and I agreed on the price, all I had to do was go to inspect it, then drive it home.

A friend of mine had offered to give Zoey and me a one-way ride to pick up the food truck, but his daughter got sick the night before we were going to leave. So I decided that Zoey and I would take the Amtrak train from Kirkwood, Missouri, to Kansas City, Missouri. What an adventure we'd have!

The next day, Zoey and I walked from our house to the train station, carrying some books and an iPad. She was excited about riding a train and asked, "How long is the train ride?"

"Almost five hours," I replied. "But we get to have lunch in the dining car, and we'll travel through Hermann, Missouri, where your cousins live!"

Zoey's beautiful blue eyes got as big as saucers. "Will they wave to us as we pass by?"

"Maybe!" I said. "I'll tell Aunt Kate what time we're passing through, and maybe they can come to the train station."

The train blew its whistle as it approached the station, and we boarded with the other westbound passengers. It was a smooth ride, and as we watched the towns pass by, we counted horses and cows, old barns, and grain silos. We waved at our cousins as they stood in the station, and we read books. After a couple of hours, the dining car opened for lunch.

"May I take you to lunch, dear lady?" I asked Zoey.

"Why, yes, kind sir," she replied. "That would be lovely."

We ate lunch in the dining car and pretended we were royalty returning home. We spent a lot of time imagining, dreaming, pretending, and laughing together because that was what Zoey loved to do.

From the train station in Kansas City, Missouri, we took an Uber car over the state line to inspect the truck. There it sat, a former BBQ truck in front of a gun shop! After completing the inspection, I settled up with the kind owner. He told us he'd gotten into the BBQ business with his dad when he was eight, and I remarked that Zoey, who was also eight, was a part of our family's starting this new business.

Then we were off to Saint Louis, with Zoey's feet dangling off the passenger jump seat. She was bundled up in a heavy coat and wore a pair of headphones to quiet the highway noise in our new, but unexpectedly loud, truck. All we could hear was the banging and clanging of the metal doors and racks in the back as we drove down Interstate 70.

Then, CRASH! Not the truck; something in the truck.

"What was that?" Zoey shouted, pulling off her headphones.

"I don't know, but it didn't sound good," I said. I took the next exit so we could pull off the highway and inspect the situation.

When we opened the door to access the back of the truck, we saw metal lids and pans spewed all over the floor. One of the cabinet latches had come undone, and all the pans had flown out. Zoey and I looked at each other, and we both started laughing our heads off.

I recently asked Zoey what her favorite part of that trip was, and she said, "Riding in the food truck!"

It was fun to relate to Zoey, and we experienced something new together. Safely out of range of any colleagues from work who could witness my less-than-professional behavior, I felt a joyful sense of freedom and adventure with her.

The name *Zoey* means *life* in Greek, which is why we gave her that name. She has been full of life since birth, and when I related to her sense of adventure and her zest for life, we etched an unforgettable day together.

On a recent fishing trip, Zoey learned to cast her fishing line. She wanted to cast it farther and farther out, so she flung it harder and harder. After one particularly hard cast, she lost her balance and fell in the lake. The water was waist-high and cold, and some algae had collected in the spot where she fell.

Poor Zoey had algae all over her and was scared after falling in. To ease her anxiety, I said, "Next time you see a big fish you want to go after, Zoey, let me know so I can jump in with you!"

Zoey's tears turned to laughter as we created yet another shared experience, which has become part of our family folklore. Now we talk about the time that Zoey jumped on the back of a giant fish and swam across the lake. Turn your own experiences into fish stories, and you'll build on your relationship.

But what if you can't relate to your daughter's interests? In that case, the best way to relate to our children sometimes is to recognize what they need and connect them with other people who can best meet those needs.

Zoey had a friend whose mother had majored in art and worked at Washington University in St. Louis. Since Grace, now an older teenager, was thinking about majoring in art history in college, this kind woman agreed to meet with Grace to explore that possibility. After the meeting, Grace shared the conversation with me.

"What kind of jobs did you talk about?" I asked.

"A museum curator and an art restorer," Grace said. "You can actually help restore pieces of historic art," she continued. Her eyes brightened and her voice lifted. I could tell she was excited about this. Since then, I've become more aware of what's going on in the art world and have had many opportunities to talk about them with Grace.

But I didn't wait until Grace was about to leave the nest to create ways to relate to her. When she was thirteen, I took her out for a special father–daughter dinner to celebrate her purity and the gift that she is now and would be to her future husband. She was all dressed up in a beautiful dress, and looking at her literally made my heart squeeze.

While we waited for our meal to arrive, I asked, "Would you allow me to be a part of your life by sharing our dreams and fears with each other?"

She looked puzzled.

"I don't want to be *that* dad," I said with urgency. "That dad that checks out of his daughter's life at thirteen and checks back in at twenty-three, just to give her away to another man. I know I won't always understand everything, and I certainly don't know everything. But if you let me, we will live with and love each other through some amazing adventures."

Grace looked a little surprised and said, "I was expecting us to have the purity talk about saving myself for marriage."

"With every good life, there's adversity and difficulties, and we'll have to overcome them together," I pressed. "Will you be willing to forgive me when I screw up and when things get hard and I don't know what to do?"

"Yes," she replied, not fully knowing what she'd just agreed to or what might lay ahead.

"You're our first child, and this is our first time going through the teenage years," I continued. "We have to learn together. It will require courageous patience and forgiveness all along the way. I may not always know how to relate to you because we're quite different in our interests, but I love the art in you, and you are my joy."

She lowered her eyes and smiled. "Thanks, Dad," she said.

"Oh, and save yourself for marriage!" I added.

I wanted Grace to know that my ultimate aim was to be a fully present, fully available father who loved and accepted her, no matter what. To do that, I needed to know her hopes and dreams, as well as her struggles and fears. For me to relate to Grace in her teen years, I needed her commitment to let me in, even when I said or did something wrong. I soon found out how much I'd need that commitment.

Philosopher Simone Weil said, "Attention is the rarest and purest form of generosity." I agree. Give your daughters the gift of your full attention. Whatever you do with them, make it special. Wrap it up, put a bow on it, or make it a special ceremony.

I'm not saying it's easy. I remember when I stood in line with Grace and her friend Ellie for the new Harry Potter ride at Universal Studios Hollywood in Orlando, Florida. The wait was four hours—for a ninety-second ride! I was tempted to complain, and I have to admit that the first hour was painfully slow. Then it dawned on me that I was being ungrateful for the gift I had. We were on vacation and could turn any time together into quality time.

I turned to Grace and Ellie and asked, "Which Harry Potter book is your favorite?"

That set them off, and they rambled on about every book and why one was better than the next.

"What's your favorite Disney character," I asked next, "and can you do an impression or sing a song from their story?"

After a few rounds of my own terrible singing, I opened the Heads Up! app that instructs you to place your smartphone on your head while you try to guess the Disney character or movie it displays from the clues that the people around you give. We got lost in that game and passed another half hour.

"If you could have any superpower, which would you choose?" I asked, trying to move the conversation away from Disney.

"I'd want to time-travel," Grace said.

"Why? Where and when would you go?" I asked.

"To London first, then Paris, then to visit all the beautiful places around the world," she said.

This started a conversation about my travels to those places and my experiences. The next three hours went by much faster, and we discovered a way to relate to one another through our imagination. We looked and acted pretty silly, and we certainly annoyed the other people who waited in line. But we now have a treasured memory that will last forever.

WHEN YOU'RE THERE, *BE* THERE

Of course, you don't have to plan spectacular outings to connect with your children. Life is full of relaxed, daily moments that are perfect opportunities to relate. In fact, there are so many opportunities that you're bound to be astounded when you start paying attention. It could be as simple as having a sandwich together at your kitchen table.

> Put away your phone, push work and other distractions out of your mind, get rid of that hurry-up attitude, and be present when you're with your daughters.

But you won't capture these moments if your body is present but your mind isn't. In other words, when you're there, *be* there. Put away your phone, push work and other distractions out of your mind, get rid of that hurry-up attitude, and be present when you're with your daughters.

I find many opportunities to relate to my girls by simply offering them hospitality—for example, preparing breakfast for Grace. Because I drove Grace to her high school every morning, she had to get up, eat breakfast, and get in the car in time for me to drop her at school and then get to work.

Most mornings, she'd dawdle and come downstairs late, put all her things in her bag, grab a water bottle and a quick bite to eat, and get in the car. I was furious at how disrespectful she was and for making me late. We typically drove the ten minutes to school in silence or with me scolding her.

One morning, I decided to start a bit earlier. I went in her room and said, "Good morning, Grace. It's time to get up. I'm making some toast. Would you like some with butter or jelly?"

"Sure," came her sleepy response. "Butter would be great."

I also filled up her water bottle so it would be ready for her to throw in her bag. When we got in the car that morning, each of us was in a better mood and able to start our day on a positive note.

Of course, I'd have loved it if she did these things for herself, but the last six months had been miserable for both of us. It wasn't rocket science to figure out that Grace wasn't a morning person. It was a small sacrifice for me to get up a little earlier and do these things for her, yet it made a major difference in our relationship that's had lasting benefits.

Now, I often wander up to Grace's room and knock on her door. "Can I come in?" I ask.

Her response is always, "Yes."

I tell her, "I need some drops of Grace to carry me today"— a favorite line from a Christian song we both like by the group For King & Country.

When my kids were little, I used to go in their rooms at night just to stare at them in their cribs, to lay my hand on their bellies to feel them breathe, or to listen to them inhale and exhale. My only desire was to be close to them. But as they got older, and my expectations for them grew and their responsibilities mounted, I found that most of the time I spent with them revolved around supervising their lives, their homework, their chores.

I've recently reverted to how I acted during their baby days. I head upstairs just to be with them. I allow my heart rate to slow down and, after a few minutes together in their rooms, they usually open up and start to talk about something important to them.

> The gift of your presence is critical; without it, you can't relate to your children. It can be grand or simple, but the important thing is to make it happen.

We usually end up by praying together. When we pray together, we relate; we share our fears and gratitude, desires and shortcomings. And by listening to each other pray, we relate better to one another because we understand one another.

The gift of your presence is critical; without it, you can't relate to your children. It can be grand or simple, but the important thing is to make it happen. Find some time to simply be with your daughter this week.

IDEAS TO IMPLEMENT

It's easier to relate to your daughters than you might think. Here are some ideas to get you going:

- Create a new Hallmark holiday by announcing to your daughter, "Today is Second Daughter Day, and since you're my second girl, we must celebrate!" Plan the adventure ahead of time, based on what she loves.

- Make a list of all the things she loves and create experiences around them. Be sure to keep the list updated because what she liked six months ago may be way behind her now.

  I made a list of each of my daughters' favorite things, a list of her dreams, a list of her fears, and so on. And I enlisted each of the two girls to help me make her list when we had time together—in the car on road trips, waiting in line at amusement parks, or grabbing a quick bite before or after an event. Keep it fun and light by dreaming and imagining with them and sharing some of your favorites, too.

  If you find that most of your adventures with your daughter revolve around your own passions and interests, go back to the list of her favorites, and make them *your* favorite things for that week, that day, that hour!

- Watch a TV show that she loves with her. Grace loves *Sherlock* and is a fan of Benedict Cumberbatch. The show itself is quite well written and interesting, and last year she invited me to watch the season opener. Zoey loves *Lab Rats*. This one was much harder for me as I tend to get sarcastic at all the whining and the name calling. But once I corrected my attitude, it was fun to watch Zoey laugh, and we even had some discussions about respect for other people. Relating with my daughter over *Lab Rats*—who knew!

- Share an experience: a concert, show, movie, sporting event, song, or video.

  Grace once played a song for me, "Be Kind to Yourself" by Andrew Peterson, during a study break, and we concentrated on the lyrics: "I love you just the way that you are, I love you and the shape of your heart, be kind to yourself." Normally, I would have asked her how her homework was going and reminded her to stay off SnapChat, NetFlix, or FaceTime. But this time, she invited me to listen to a song that meant something to her. Now it means something to me as well.

Zoey asked to see the movie *Hidden Figures* with me. When I asked why, she said, "It's about women who helped launch the first astronauts into space." Zoey (*life*) is all about setting her mind to do something and going after it. There's nothing she can't do.

Relating on such a level may occur in unexpected and fun ways. Be open and available for these moments.

- Read what she's reading. Find out her favorite book, or author, or topic. When I read *Divergent* before the midnight premiere that I took Grace and her friend to see, it allowed me to share an experience with Grace that I would have otherwise missed. Zoey and I read *Goldilicious* together—which led to our fantasies about Zoeylicious—and we created fun stories around that. Zoey even wrote a short story about Zoeylicious for a school project, and we had a lot of fun reading it together.

- Download a cool new app. Even if technology isn't your thing, this can be a lot of fun and can inject laughter into the relationship. I downloaded *FaceSym* and had a hilarious time with Grace and Zoey. After you take a photo of your face, the app applies the photo to one side of your face to create your perfectly symmetrical face—which makes you look completely different. I find that when I relate frequently to my kids in fun and silly ways, it helps balance the times when I have to hold them accountable to their responsibilities like chores and homework.

- Schedule a venting session with your daughter, but set some boundaries beforehand, for example, a maximum time of five minutes or less, no name calling, and no cursing. During her sophomore year in high school, Grace, who isn't one for drama, was having a tough time with some of her friends and just needed to vent. I invited her to take a walk around the block one night to share those frustrations, and she did. Talking helped her release some of her pent-up, negative energy and helped me to get invited into her life more often.

- If you've tried to be creative and find that your adventures lack sizzle or are not extraordinary by any measure, ask your craziest friends (or your child's craziest friends) what they'd do to amp it up! Always focus on what would make for an extraordinary adventure for your daughter, not you.

- As your girls get into the older elementary years, mix it up a bit and create a little adversity for yourselves. Next time you're out with them, ask them to navigate you home all by themselves—no help from electronics or GPS devices. Ask questions to guide them along and help them think through how to find their way home, but don't give any answers. Afterward, talk about how the experience made them feel, and ask what the most challenging and fun things were in the experience. You can learn a lot about how to relate to one another when you create situations where you need each other's help.

WHAT IS REQUIRED OF ME?

Growth comes from personal examination, so if you want to learn to relate to your daughter, ask yourself these questions:

- Am I fully available and present for times when she wants to talk?

- Do I create or offer ideas about how to relate to things that matter to her?

- How often do I suspend my parental role and simply listen and learn more about my daughter?

- How often do I talk about her performance or what she needs to do, rather than simply listening to and loving her?

Grace has taught me the value of simply being, whether through her drawing a sketch of her brother or playing a cool new song on her ukulele. It's helped me move from being an enforcer of rules and a collector of achievements to becoming a fully present father who appreciates the art in her.

If you hear your daughter say, "Ask Mom. Dad wouldn't know," it's a sign that you're too disconnected. Now is the time to change that. Knock on her door and ask if you can be with her for a few minutes—without phones, music, anything. Simply be. Ask no questions, and remain silent until your daughter speaks first. See what happens!

If this is too strange or new for you or your daughter, ask some simple open-ended questions about something that interests her. Is she open to your questions, or is she suspicious? Tell her that you want to get to know her better and be an ongoing part of her life. She still may not like it, but you'll have shown her that she's important to you, even if you sense some resistance.

It's my job to relate to my daughters, not the other way around. They've never been my age, never been a parent, never been a man, and never gone to college or to work. Even though I've never been a girl, I've been their age.

Your daughters want you to take the effort to get to know them as they are—not some manufactured version of who you want them to be. They want you to know and love them exactly as they are.

And this isn't a once-and-done kind of thing. It's ongoing. Stay sharp and be aware of the changes that take place in them from week to week and month to month. Otherwise, you'll find yourself right back at the beginning.

Of course, these ideas can work for boys, too, but girls seem to be a special challenge for fathers. The ultimate goal is to make all your children feel *known*. When you know them, you can relate to them. And when you know them, you value them for their unique ways of being and presenting themselves to the world.

PART 2

Children Need to Feel *Valued*

When you're **VALUED**, you feel important, and you know that you matter to someone. More deeply, you feel cherished. When children feel valued, they have a strong sense of self-worth from which their self-esteem can develop in a safe and healthy setting.

It starts with listening to your kids and making sure they feel heard—which says that you value their words, thoughts, feelings, opinions, and beliefs. While you don't have to agree with them, you need to acknowledge and validate them. Legitimize what your child is saying, and let him know you understand. *Feeling* valued comes from genuinely *being* valued, and giving your time and full attention is the currency.

Children also feel valued when they play a role in the family that only they can fill. In our household, we rely on each child for something and depend on them to complete their jobs on a regular basis. It could be as simple as setting the table, clearing the dishes, or emptying the dishwasher. Each of our roles, duties, and chores creates an interdependent relationship in the family, and the kids develop a sense of accomplishment, self-worth, and value to the family team.

> Each of our roles, duties, and chores creates an interdependent relationship in the family, and the kids develop a sense of accomplishment, self-worth, and value to the family team.

But it's all too easy to build barriers and make excuses that can prevent our children from feeling valued. By understanding them better, we can consciously work to avoid falling into that trap.

CHAPTER 5

◆

I get so frustrated and angry with my kids!

It was a Saturday morning, and I was fixing breakfast for two-year-old Grace. She sat by my feet and played contentedly with some wooden spoons. After awhile, she stood up, walked to the metal garbage can, and started banging on the lid. It was really loud—annoyingly loud.

I walked over to her and whispered, "Gracie, please stop banging. Mommy is still asleep, and we don't want to wake her up."

She stopped for an instant, then started the ruckus again.

I walked over to her a second time and said, "Honey, please, please stop banging on the can. Try banging on the floor."

Not as much fun. She banged on the floor once or twice, then went back to the metal can. The third time I got down on my knee to meet her at eye level.

"Gracie, *please* stop banging."

She looked at me, then at the spoon, then at the can, and then back at me. Then she threw her head back and let out the most diabolical little laugh I'd ever heard.

"HA HA HA HA HA!" she cried out and began banging on the can with the spoon again.

Welcome to parenting, I thought. I felt frustrated and helpless, and I had no idea what to do next.

I've been in this situation a lot. When I try to correct my kids, try to teach them something, or try to get them to do something, it's like they can't hear me. I feel like they don't respect me, and it makes me want to tear my hair out!

I've tried several approaches to get their cooperation, most of them unsuccessful. I've tried to be more patient. I've sought to understand the situation before I react. I've attempted to reason with them, and I've tried to help them understand me and what I've asked them to do. None of these has been effective.

I don't like to wait, and that's what the word *patience* meant to me: waiting. It means I have to bear or endure something, or I have to persevere, all of which involve a good deal of energy and some level of pain, discomfort, or irritation. And I have to do it all without complaining or losing my temper. Patience doesn't come easy for me.

I like the phrase *courageous patience,* and I remember when I first experienced what it really meant. Grace didn't wake up in time for school one morning. I left for work, and my wife had to get to early appointments north of the city. So Grace had to walk a little over a mile to her school. By the time she arrived, she'd missed all but fifteen minutes of her first class. As luck would have it, they had an in-class essay that day, and her teacher gave her a zero for the assignment.

Wouldn't you know, it was the same day that we had parent–teacher conferences. When my wife and I met with Grace's first-period teacher, she shook her head and said, "I don't meet many parents like you."

"What do you mean?" I asked.

"Parents who have the courage to make their kids walk to school," she said.

"Maybe from where you sit, it looks like courage," I told her, "but it sure doesn't feel like that to us!"

> Courageous patience means that you're brave enough to make tough decisions and see them through—even if there are negative consequences for your child.

Grace's zero stuck. We didn't ask the teacher for any special favors; we simply accepted and respected her decision.

We'd exercised courageous patience. Courageous patience means that you're brave enough to make tough decisions and see them through—even if there are negative consequences for your child. No one wants to see their children struggle, but we must make courageous decisions so they can learn from their own choices.

Exercising courageous patience requires you to let *your dreams* for your child die and allow *your child's dreams* to live. I realized that when I get angry and frustrated with my children, it's because what they've done—or not done—jeopardized *my* dreams for them—my dreams that they'll get the best grades, go to the best schools, have the best opportunities.

But our job as parents isn't to shield our kids from consequences; it's to let them experience these pains in small ways while they're still at home and under our care. When we allow them to experience both the positive and negative consequences of their actions, we show that we value them, even though it may be painful at the time.

Our job isn't to shield our kids from consequences; it's to let them experience these pains in small ways while they're still at home and under our care.

I've found that if I try to figure out what's going on with my child when *I* get the most frustrated and angry, I can respond better the next time. If you want to do the same, here are some things for you to think about whenever you feel frustrated with your kids:

- What is your child's frame of mind?

- Did something lead up to this? Who were they with? What were they doing?

- What is your child struggling with? What are you struggling with?

- What is your child seeking right now?

- What does your child need that you can provide?

Answering these questions always helps me gain perspective. Of course, it doesn't make sense to discipline a two-year-old who only wants to have fun and make noise. In that case, I was perhaps the one who needed to pull back, let Grace act her age, and be silly right along with her.

BACK OFF

My kids don't always need my instruction, as I discussed earlier. When Grace was struggling with anxiety and depression, I was deeply frustrated because I wanted to understand the difference between normal teenage behavior and her symptoms of depression. But I neglected to ask myself, "What does she need?" I regret that I missed opportunities to simply be with her until her anxiety and depression subsided.

A friend shed light on the value of just being with someone when he told me about the Jewish practice of sitting *shiva*. He explained that, as part of the mourning process, people visit the home of a bereaved family and simply sit with them. There's no need to speak; they simply sit among the family and other friends as a sign of love for both the family and the deceased.

I've drawn on this concept several times when Grace was in her darkest depression and there was nothing I could do to help her except *be* with her. My silent sitting lasted from ten minutes to an hour. That's what love looked like for Grace in those moments and how she felt valued.

I once got frustrated with Luc—actually, hurt—when he told me he didn't want to practice pitching or catching with me anymore.

"I want to be a better pitcher," Luc said, "so I want to take lessons from a pitching coach."

"Are you willing to put in the practice?"

"Yes, but I want to do it with a coach."

"I get that," I said. "But you'll have to practice between lessons, and I'm willing to catch for you."

"OK," Luc replied, "but can we just play catch sometimes without you giving me a bunch of instructions?"

Ouch. On the one hand, it hurt that Luc didn't want my instruction. But on the other hand, I appreciated that he'd had the courage to tell me. Then it struck me: *How can Luc feel valued when I constantly tell him what to do?*

MAYBE THE PROBLEM IS YOU

When dealing with my kids, or anyone else for that matter, I'm half the equation. I can't look only at what's going on with my child; I have to examine myself and identify my own trigger points.

One morning, as Zoey was making her breakfast, she spilled the milk. No big deal. That's what kids do, right? A good dad would have helped her clean it up, or at least handed her a towel. But not me.

"Zoey!" I shouted. "Be careful! Clean that up now!"

That evening, when my wife and I were out on a date night, she asked, "Why have you been so angry lately?"

I thought a moment and then said, "I don't know why I've had such a short fuse lately. What do you think?"

"Well, you've got an injured Achilles tendon and haven't been able to run with your buddies lately," she said. "Could that be part of it?"

Megan's answer struck a chord. Maybe my anger was because I couldn't exercise the way I wanted and I was losing touch with my friends. I could see how that would contribute to my short fuse.

Here's the thing: When you're sick or injured, give yourself a break. Recognize that you're not your best self and that things are going to be different for awhile. Even when you try to hide it, that anger is under the surface. The key is to recognize what's going on, so you can manage your emotions.

I decided I could get through my "no-run, no-fun" time— and stay active and feel healthier—by swimming or taking up light cycling As for my angry outbursts, Megan suggested that I give myself some time and distance when I felt the spark of my short fuse. I decided I'd remove myself from frustrating situations by going upstairs or outside until I could respond appropriately—kind of like giving myself a "time out."

I realized another trigger for my bad temper. My temper also flared when my schedule was too tight or I was overwhelmed by tasks. The remedy was simple. I combed through my calendar and to-do list, eliminating nonessential appointments and tasks. It was fun crossing off things I didn't like anyway. I immediately resigned from a board I'd been on for over ten years, and I turned down a request to consult for a business that I'd been debating for some time.

When I resigned from the board, I could see other areas where I'd fallen into a rut. At work, I'd allowed my schedule to become routine when I actually like to work with others to create new things. So I eliminated or delegated the routine tasks, freeing up time to engage with a team of colleagues on new, creative projects. When I turned down the consulting offer, I suggested people who often were more skilled or qualified than me; it felt good to recommend them.

> My temper had damaged my relationships with my kids. My angry outbursts and extreme frustration were wrong, and my behavior was my fault, not theirs.

Megan also suggested that she text me a heads-up on the situation at home before I left the office each afternoon. By cutting out surprises and allowing me to mentally prepare for the evening ahead, her texts also let me get in the mindset to respond appropriately to our children rather than overreact.

But my temper had already damaged my relationships with my kids. My angry outbursts and extreme frustration were wrong, and my behavior was my fault, not theirs. At dinner one night, I had my opportunity to apologize.

"I am sorry I've been so short-tempered and angry lately," I confessed. "I've been overreacting to small things, and I apologize for that."

"That's OK, Dad. We forgive you," Zoey replied sweetly.

"No problem, Dad," Luc chimed in.

"I forgive you, too, Dad," Grace confirmed.

"There's no excuse for it," I confessed, "but I'm really angry because I'm not getting what I want. Sounds like I'm a two-year-old, doesn't it? I'm mad that I can't run and be with my friends. But now that I see it, I'm going to work hard to improve."

I didn't realize the huge impact that apologizing to my kids would have on them. It gave them a chance to model forgiveness to my genuine apology. In addition, they learned that my anger was about me not getting what I want, letting them see that I'd been selfish.

TRICKS UP YOUR SLEEVE

Of course, life has a way of punching your buttons when you're least prepared. So I keep a couple of tricks up my sleeve to diffuse tense situations.

I pulled one of these tricks out one afternoon when my wife and I arrived home to the sounds of Grace and Luc screaming at each other. This was new for them, and they kept shouting even after I'd joined them in the living room.

I sent Luc upstairs for a few minutes to calm down and then turned to Grace. She was so worked up that she was shaking and crying. I stood face-to-face with her and gently held her hands.

"Match my breath," I told Grace. "Just try to match my breath. Innnnnnn. Outttttttt. Innnnnnn. Outttttttt."

When she finally started to take in the long breaths, I said, "Squeeze my hands, Grace." I wanted to help her release some of her worked-up energy so she could compose herself.

Later, Grace, Luc, and I sat together upstairs and talked about the problem.

"So what happened?" I asked.

"I was upset because I wanted to change the music and Luc didn't," Grace explained.

"I was listening to the music first," Luc replied in a slightly louder voice.

"Hold on, hold on," I said. "Each of you can tell me what happened from your perspective, but the goal here is for you to understand the other person, not to blame them. OK?"

> What would our childrens' lives be like if they didn't have the skills or knowledge to manage their emotions and deescalate conflict?

After Grace and Luc had told the facts as they saw them, I said, "Now it's time to apologize to each other."

"Sorry for getting so angry, Luc," Grace offered.

"I'm sorry, too," Luc responded.

"What can we learn from this," I asked, "so it doesn't happen again? Maybe we need some ground rules."

We talked about respect, listening, and letting others speak first and fully. We agreed that shouting and name-calling were off limits, as was the use of foul language. Forgiveness was also in the mix, and the kids said it was important to apologize. These became our rules: respect, listen, confirm your understanding, no shouting, proper language, and apologize.

I don't pretend that similar things haven't happened since.

But when they occur, I take charge. It's my job to teach my kids how to deal with their frustration and anger.

Of course, I have to model good behavior myself. But I also need to have mature discussions with them about what behavior is acceptable, and that won't work if I'm frustrated and angry, too. What would our children's lives be like if they didn't have the skills or knowledge to manage their emotions and deescalate conflict?

One afternoon, Grace, my wife, and I were grabbing a quick bite to eat after an appointment with Grace's doctor.

"I'm so mad at you and God for all of this," Grace said, referring to her depression and anxiety.

"Why are you angry at God?" I asked.

"Because He allowed this to happen to me," she said.

"And why are you mad at Mom and me?"

"I've been feeling bad for a long time," she said, "and you guys didn't do anything! You're the parents. You should know these things!"

It was like a slap in the face and a punch in the stomach all at once. Our child was berating us for the signs we'd missed. It was a gut-wrenching cry for help, and we'd misread her symptoms. The words still ring in my ears: "You should know these things!"

"I'm really sorry, Grace," I said, "but we don't know everything. I know we didn't see it for a long time, but once we knew about the problem, we got the best help for you that we could find. And we've educated ourselves on how to support you.

"We noticed you were acting differently," I continued, "but we thought it was normal teenager stuff. My natural response was to say 'Suck it up'—which I now know was the worst thing I could've said. I'm really sorry, Grace."

Grace calmed down. And although she didn't formally accept my apology, it was evident that we'd entered a new phase of our relationship with her. Megan and I got the message: to be better parents, we needed to be better communicators.

IDEAS TO IMPLEMENT

- Before you jump in and try to fix your kids, step back and observe the situation. Assume that you're part of the problem. If you can't see that, ask your kids. They'll tell you.

- Let your kids act their age and express their feelings. Help them articulate their feelings if they get stuck.

- Stop telling your kids what to do all the time and offer them a balanced relationship that includes fun for fun's sake.

WHAT IS REQUIRED OF ME?

Making your children feel valued requires you to be more present in their lives and to find times when you can simply be together. It also requires you to be aware that you may be part of the problem.

Sometimes it's a good idea to confide in other dads to get an objective perspective or another view about what's happening with your child. This means you'll not only have to be vulnerable, but respect your child's

> When I'm frustrated and angry with my kids, it's my problem, not theirs. How could my children possibly feel valued when I stomp all over their hearts with anger?

confidentiality and insist that the person you confide in does, too. It's hard to be open and vulnerable about family matters, but every family struggles in some way; we're better parents when we can rely on one another.

When I'm frustrated and angry with my kids, it's my problem, not theirs. How could my children possibly feel valued when I stomp all over their hearts with anger? Kids do dumb and frustrating things, and everyone blows a gasket once in awhile. But when that happens, to show that I value my kids, I must apologize, talk through the situation, and agree how I'll handle it better the next time.

CHAPTER 6

◆

I don't know where to start.

If you want to make your kids feel valued but don't know where to start, take a look at your feet. That's where you start. Right here, right now, right where you stand. Start with the big things, and work your way to the more personal things.

START AT HOME

Home is where the heart is, so demonstrate that you value your children by making your home a safe haven and creating a sense of belonging. Start by making your house feel safe and secure.

> Demonstrate that you value your children by making your home a safe haven and creating a sense of belonging.

We live in Saint Louis, Missouri, and every year tornadoes and warning sirens are a rite of springtime. To make our children feel safe and secure, Megan and I created a family plan for tornadoes that we practiced with the kids. One year, the five of us went to the basement and hunkered down in the spare bedroom with our dog and cat. We all ended up falling asleep and woke up in the morning together, safe, and sound. We created a memory *and* practiced our plan.

You may not have tornadoes where you live, but any home can have a fire. Create a fire escape plan and practice it. Take the plan and your practice seriously, and give everyone in the family a role to play.

If you want to keep things on the lighter side, have an indoor campout and pretend you have to survive the night without electricity. Give everyone a responsibility to help the family get through the blackout. One person can be responsible for food, another for water, another for light (flashlights or candles), and another for shelter and warmth (sleeping bags). The goal is to create an experience that bonds you as a family and communicates that everyone is not only valuable but also vital!

VALUE YOUR TEAM

Most people go through life with three basic questions:

- Who am I?
- Why am I here?
- Where do I belong?

Your children ask these questions, too. The most obvious answer to the first question for them is, "I'm a child." We all enter the world as a child: a child of your mother; a child of your father. If we're fortunate, we're taught that we're a child of God.

Early on, being a child means being totally dependent on others—primarily parents and caregivers, the people who meet our needs. Beyond meeting our basic needs to eat, sleep, and be changed, our parents are responsible for making us feel safe and secure.

People long to be part of something bigger than themselves, and children want and need a strong sense of family and togetherness. You can foster this and have some fun with it, like our family did when we formed the Bean Team.

CREATE FAMILY TRADITIONS

Traditions are the stories, shared activities, and experiences that we pass down from one generation to the next. Traditions, particularly family traditions, provide a source of identity and strengthen the family bond. These bundles

> If your family doesn't have any traditions, create a tradition *now*— big or small, simple or complex, frequent or infrequent.

of memories and values are also a vehicle for passing on our cultural or religious heritage. And traditions also provide a seasonal rhythm to our family unit.

If your family doesn't have any traditions, create a tradition *now*! The beauty of traditions is that they can be big or small, simple or complex, frequent or infrequent, so long as they're shared and enjoyed by your family. Here are some ideas.

- Pick a seasonal tradition that your family can celebrate. For example, every summer we go to a drive-in movie. They're hard to find these days, but there's one in our area. We pack the van with blankets and pillows, and fill a bag with everyone's favorite snacks to munch on during the show. The kids dress in their PJs, so they can get to bed quickly when we get home.

- Establish a tradition to serve others as a family. Volunteer regularly at the local community center or a local nonprofit group that interests your children. Or go on a mission trip together. When you serve together, you share experiences and build memories that forge bonds that can't be broken.

One year I went to New Orleans with Luc's youth choir. After they sang at a couple of retirement homes, the kids looked forward to dinner in the French Quarter, followed by a ghost tour. The energy on the bus was high, particularly about the ghost tour. Mid-day, the choir director got a call from the New Orleans mission, which asked the youth choir to perform there that evening. There had been a mix-up by their previous director, who'd never confirmed the date, so it wasn't on the choir's calendar. The evening plan was for the kids to go to dinner and take a ghost tour.

She let the kids decide.

"The whole purpose of this trip is about singing at the mission," one of the kids immediately said. A second echoed the sentiment, and the kids decided to cancel dinner so they could go where they were needed.

This particular week was the hottest ever in New Orleans, and the mission wasn't air conditioned. Some of the kids looked like they might pass out, but none of them complained.

After the trip, Luc told me that his favorite part of the trip was when they sang there, and I admit, I was proud that they had chosen to serve others instead of following their own desires. But as luck would have it, there was a later start time for the ghost tour, and we got to experience that, as well.

- Plan and prepare a weekly meal together as a family, rotating responsibility for choosing the menu. Then plan the shopping, chopping, cooking, and mopping together, and ensure that everyone has a job to do. Rotate the jobs from week to week as well.

One night, Zoey, Luc, and I made Thai food for dinner. Zoey and I looked up the recipe, and the three of us went to the store to buy the ingredients. When we got there, we turned our shopping outing into a treasure hunt.

"Luc, you track down the coconut milk, and Zoey and I will grab the curry and lemon grass," I suggested. "Meet us in the ice cream aisle when you're done."

After we picked up some cookie dough ice cream to go with our exotic ingredients, we headed home.

"I'll get the chicken started," Zoey shouted as she bounded from the car into the house.

"Luc, will you chop the lemon grass and vegetables for the soup?" I asked.

"Sure!" He was on it.

With the smell of curry wafting through the air, I asked, "What do you think it would be like to live in Thailand?"

"Where's Thailand?" Zoey asked.

"It's in Asia," Luc explained.

We imagined living in the hot, humid summers in Thailand and munching on curry chicken.

Our meal was delicious, but it was the time we spent together—shopping for the ingredients, preparing and cooking the food, and cleaning up afterward—that made it so special.

If it's hard for you to figure out a new family tradition, pick one of my suggestions and go for it. I've met a number of men who delegate much of this work to their spouses, and then they wonder why they don't have strong relationships with their kids. If you want a relationship with your kids, you must engage with them. To build a team, you've got to lead the team! Lead them in family traditions.

VALUE ALL YOUR MEMBERS

We went through a period when Zoey fought us on everything we did. When we needed her to get in the car to take Grace or Luc to a rehearsal or practice, she whined and said she didn't want to go. Once when we went to a restaurant that we all liked, Zoey refused to order her meal, saying she wasn't hungry. Another time, she flat-out refused to do one of her chores; "I'm not doing it," she announced firmly.

Shortly after that, Megan and I slipped away for a romantic night at an out-of-town B&B. We drove to a remote village with a quaint Victorian house. It reminded me of New England, where I'd spent much of my youth. After a day filled with cycling, shopping, and wine tasting, we returned to the B&B after midnight and slept past the breakfast hour. We woke up to the smell of coffee and fresh pastries, but the clock told us it was past the time when they served breakfast.

We were the only ones who had stayed at the house that

night, and the couple who ran it had made everything just for us. And they wanted us to enjoy it. So we shared a quiet breakfast and, as often is the case, our conversation turned to our children.

"Can you pass the butter, please?" Megan asked, as she broke open the homemade croissant.

"Have you noticed that Zoey's behavior has changed lately?" I asked, biting into my second cinnamon roll.

"Yeah, I think she may be going through a phase," she said.

"What is it? What do you think is going on? She's so unhappy and uncooperative whenever we go out or when we ask her to do something," I said. "Is she having too much screen time?"

"I think she's tired of being dragged around all the time to everything for everyone else," Megan said. "She has no say, no voice."

"Then we need to change that," I said. "We have to give her more of a voice."

We had another cup of coffee and came up with a few ideas.

"Let's ask Zoey to pick the next game or movie on Friday family night," Megan suggested.

"Good idea. We can also let her choose the restaurant the next time we eat out before or after one of Grace's or Luc's events," I said.

At first, Megan and I thought that Zoey had been acting out because she didn't get what she wanted. But when we examined each situation, we realized that she had no voice in our family.

Zoey had no choices. She had no say in her own life because we constantly dragged her to all of the other kids' activities. Her days were spent doing what she was told to do, wearing what she was told to wear, and going where she was told to go. The times she was most belligerent were when she didn't want to do what we asked. Actually, we'd never really asked her.

Put another way, Zoey didn't feel valued.

We were determined to create ways to give Zoey a voice in the family and allow her to make some decisions, and we enlisted the cooperation of Grace and Luc. We had a Friday night tradition of ordering pizza and then watching a movie or playing a game together. The next Friday night, we let Zoey pick the activity and also decide where we'd eat when we went out for dinner that evening.

Once Zoey began to feel that she was a valued member of the family, her behavior and attitude changed completely. She was part of the team again.

LEARN THEIR LOVE LANGUAGE

Maybe you've tried to communicate with your kids by using their slang and terminology, but a far more effective way to reach them is to learn their *love language*. The concept of love languages was developed by author Gary Chapman, and Megan and I were introduced to it in a small group for young married couples at our church.

Chapman defines the five love languages as follows:

- **Words of affirmation**—Love is offered and received through words of affection, praise, or appreciation.

- **Acts of service**—Actions, rather than words, are demonstrations of love.

- **Receiving gifts**—Giving and receiving gifts is how love is expressed and received.

- **Quality time**—Having undivided, undistracted attention is how love is given and received.

- **Physical touch**—A hug or embrace, a kiss, a touch of a hand, a pat on the back, and a hand on the shoulder are ways of expressing affection through physical touch.

To figure out how each of your children expresses love, watch them and notice their patterns. Compare your observations with what others observe—your spouse and the children's grandparents, aunts, and uncles. And for age-specific tools to help you to identify your children's love language, visit www.5lovelanguages.com.

> For age-specific tools to help you to identify your children's love language, visit www.5lovelanguages.com.

Early on, we learned that Grace's love language is words of affirmation, followed by quality time, and then receiving gifts. Because we value Grace, we speak her language. We use our spoken words to lift her up and write notes to her on a regular basis, always about meaningful and authentic subjects. After she passed her driving test on the first try—including perfect parallel parking—we praised her and told her how diligent she was to study for the test and put in the driving hours needed to pass.

Grace and I connect the most and have the best conversations in the car after I pick her up from choir practice. Many nights, we sit in the car in the driveway once we're home because we're still talking. I let her love and joy overflow, and I simply listen. Quality time is what love looks like for Grace. By sharing these private times with her, I show that I value her.

Grace was two when Luc was born, and we gave her a new little shirt as a gift from him. We lived in Belgium at the time, and Megan had a shirt made for Grace that said "La Grande Soeur," which means "The Big Sister." In a photo of Grace wearing that shirt that remains precious to us, Grace is lying down next to tiny little Luc, with the most beautiful expression of love and gratitude on her face.

Luc's love language is words of affirmation and physical touch, followed by receiving gifts. We give him a healthy dose of written notes and verbal praise, and we also make sure to hug him when we see him. I go out of my way to give Luc a hug in the morning and before he goes to bed. Now that he's a teenager and self-conscious about displays of affection, I give him a bro-hug when he's out with friends.

Luc is a lot like me: he loves competitive sports. But more than the competition, Luc enjoys the camaraderie of being part of a team. Now that I no longer yell instructions to him from the sidelines, he loves it when I come to his games to be his encourager. When he was little, we used to wrestle to fulfill his need for physical touch. But now that he's a teenager, and after he pulled the single-leg lift takedown move on me, I suggested that we just fist-bump, to avoid trips to the ER!

Zoey is all about words of affirmation, receiving gifts, and physical touch. She is a full-on competitor and loves sports, especially softball. We frequently talk about her goals for a particular game or for the season, and Megan and I offer her praise based on that information. When I praise her after a great practice or after one of our catching sessions, she lights up from head to toe. I try to be specific in my words of affirmation to Zoey; for example, I tell her how great her fastball and curve ball are coming along.

Whenever we surprise Zoey with a small gift that is both personal and relevant, she's ecstatic. She treasures a hand-knit, colorful purse that I bought her while I was in Guatemala on a business trip. The bonus is that now she wants to join me on a mission trip some day.

Zoey and I have our own special handshake, high five, fist-bump routine that no one else knows about. It's an example of physical touch that creates another intimate bond between me and my daughter.

If you want your kids to feel valued, find their love language and learn to express your love to them in that way. The more personal, relevant, and authentic your efforts are, the greater the rewards will be for both you and your children.

> If you want your kids to feel valued, find their love language and learn to express your love to them in that way.

I'll leave you with a strange, but true, story about love languages. When I first discovered that my wife's love language was *acts of service*, I used to joke that vacuuming the living room was foreplay. While that's kind of funny, it's not far from the truth. When I do something for Megan that's on her to-do list, particularly if it's something she doesn't like to do, it goes a long way!

IDEAS TO IMPLEMENT

Consider borrowing some of the ways in which I show my kids that I value them:

- I put a note in Grace's lunch or send her a text to tell her how much I like to hear about her hopes and dreams, as well as her fears and disappointments. I tell her I enjoy the artist in her and that I'm proud that she works hard to be exceptional.

- I took Luc to his first NCAA tournament game, where we shared the fun of cheering on our favorite team. Going to a special event with just one of your children—and focusing all your thoughts, energy, and attention on that child during the outing—makes your child feel valued.

- To feed Zoey's sense of adventure and her imagination, we created a story together that we add to every night, called Zoeylicious. It's about the adventures of Zoeylicious, a princess who lives in the Kingdom of the Clouds. Night after night after night, the story grew until Zoey and I had built a special kingdom that is only hers and mine.

What Is Required of Me?

The more you make your children feel *known*, the more they will feel *valued*. First and foremost, spend as much one-on-one time as it takes to get to know each of them—and start now! Be adventurous enough to try new things and to create new traditions.

Even if something feels awkward or doesn't work out exactly as you planned, the fact that you invested your time and energy in the effort will speak volumes to your child. When you create special experiences with them, they will, at some level, feel valued. And to help their self-esteem and self-worth grow, learn their love language and then relate to each of your kids in the way they're wired to receive.

CHAPTER 7

◆

I don't have enough
time for this.

I was on carpool duty, and after rounding up our three kids from their activities, I started a conversation on the way home.

"Today, I heard about a professor at Princeton who gives his new students an interesting assignment each semester," I said. "They have to go on a media fast for thirty days and then write a paper about the impact that media has on their lives."

"What's a media fast?" Luc asked.

"It's like any other fast," I answered. "When you're on a fast, you eliminate something from your life for a specific period of time. These students are on a media fast, so that means no TV, no movies, no social media, no computer games, and anything else like that." I paused before dropping the bombshell: "What would you think about our family doing that?"

I expected an explosive reaction.

"I'd totally do that," Grace said without any hesitation. I think she liked the idea of doing something that college students did.

"I would, too!" Luc agreed.

Not to be left out, Zoey chimed in, "Me, too!"

I was stunned—but thrilled that they had agreed. Who doesn't long to yank the phone out of a texting teenager's hand to have a little eye contact and intelligent conversation every now and then?

The timing seemed perfect because it was just before Lent. So we all agreed to fast from media for those forty days.

But right away, I realized that I'd put myself in a bind. The NCAA March Madness basketball tournament, when I'm normally glued to the TV, was approaching. *I got myself into this. There's no turning back now.*

Here's how the first four weeks went down:

> Our major family takeaway was that it's important to dedicate time together to things that matter most because it makes us all feel valued.

Week 1—The kids moaned and groaned about the TV shows they were missing, from *Supernatural* to *Lab Rats* to basketball games. Our reading time, however, increased significantly.

Week 2—We had more time on our hands than ever. Although we weren't the most productive, we started to be more present with one another instead of escaping into our individual screens.

Week 3—We did more things as a family: we played games, went for walks, and planned and experienced new adventures.

Week 4—I decided that just because I couldn't watch TV, it didn't mean that I had to miss March Madness. So I bought tickets and went to two games—one with Luc and one with Zoey. On the drive down, we debated whether we were cheating because the game was televised, but we decided that going to the games with each other was the goal of the fast, and it was nothing like watching it on TV. It was awesome, and my two kids and I created lifelong memories.

When the forty days were over, we reflected on the experience just like the Princeton students did. Grace enjoyed her freedom from social media and from always being "on." She said she hadn't realized how much social media influenced her—she didn't like it. Luc and Zoey liked having time to do some things as a family that we hadn't done in awhile. But they said they wished we'd made a list of alternative activities before we started the fast so the first two weeks of detox wouldn't have been so hard. Our major family takeaway was that it's important to dedicate time together to things that matter most—like face-to-face conversations and going on outings—because it makes us all feel valued.

You *Do* Have Time

You've heard that you always have time for the things that are important to you, and I agree with that. But as men and fathers, we also have responsibilities and claims on our time that are somewhat inflexible. That's why I think it's useful to look at time from three perspectives: capacity, priority, and elasticity.

Capacity

You can measure time in seconds, minutes, hours, days, months, and years. Life, however, is actually measured in moments—moments of connection, which have a weighted value. When your calendar is full and there's no capacity for more, you have to take something off to create space for a new and intentional activity.

Take a look at how you spend your time. Get a piece of paper and, on the left side, list each hour in a vertical column. Next to each hour, write down what you did that day—for example, work out, eat, drive to work, teleconference 1, meeting 1, lunch, meeting 2, teleconference 2, drive home, eat dinner, drop kids off, pick kids up, go for walk with wife and kids (this would be nice!), watch TV, and so on. If this is too difficult to remember, try logging your activity for the next day or two.

7-8am	• Shower, change, eat; Drive to work
8-12noon	• Work
12-1pm	• Lunch
1-5pm	• Work
5-6pm	• Drive home/gym
6-7pm	• Workout/Run with Meg
7-8pm	• Make dinner with Zoey & play rummy with her
8-9pm	• Watch end of XU/Butler game with Luc
9-10pm	• Watch 30 min of Youtube videos with Grace
10-11pm	• Read/Bed

Next, evaluate. How much time do you spend with each of your children? How can you make that time quality time? Do you *intentionally* plan specific times with your wife and each of your kids, or is it catch-as-catch-can, so the time you spend with them is an afterthought?

I used to keep two schedules: the schedule I created for myself that was all about me, and the schedule for my wife and kids that Megan managed. Since I was my own priority back then, I looked at the family schedule as if it were a menu of kids' items and I could choose the ones I wanted to be part of.

I bet if you looked at your schedule, you'd be surprised at how many hours you spend on yourself in a week. "You" time includes any and all time that doesn't include your wife or children—so, yes, it includes your work hours. Even if you serve others, count that as "you" time as well.

What percentage of your time during a week do you spend with your wife and children? 10 percent? 25 percent? 50 percent? There's no right answer and no judgment here. This is simply an exercise to point out where and how you spend your time, so that you can *do* something different to find more time for them.

Now look at your "you" list. What can you eliminate? Can you cut down or cut out TV? (You can always watch your favorite shows on HULU or Netflix when the kids are grown or after they're in bed.) Could you use some of that TV time to fix dinner with your kids; clean up afterward; or go for a walk, run, or bike ride with them? Where can you carve out some quality time with your wife and each child every week? Could you plan a weekly lunch with your wife or with one of your kids? Summer is a great time to have a workday picnic!

To demonstrate that I value my children, I set aside a specific time each week to sit down with Megan to help plan and be a proactive part of our kids' schedules. Megan helps me better understand the needs of each child, so I know how to support them and help them feel valued. If you're a single parent, you might connect with one of your children's other caregivers to conduct this exercise.

Megan and I both like sushi, and I wanted these family strategy sessions to be fun. So I invited her to have sushi with me at our local high-end grocery store (which actually serves great food). Once a week, or at worst once every two weeks, we meet there for our sushi logistic sessions. (By the way, this dinner session doesn't count as our date night!)

Priority

> If you want your kids to feel valued, you have to make each of them a priority—*every week*. This means scheduling time with them before you put other things on your calendar.

I used to think if I treated each of my children the same, all would be well. So I took each one to a baseball game, to a show, on a walk, or out to dinner. But my children are different ages and at different stages of life, and they have different interests, joys, and struggles. By connecting regularly with Megan about what each of our children need, I can better prioritize where and how to spend time with each one.

If you want your kids to feel valued, you have to make each of them a priority—*every week*. This literally means scheduling time with them before you put other things on your calendar. (A word of caution: make the time and attention that you give each of your children roughly the same, so one child doesn't feel less valued than the others.)

I had to get creative to do this and still get everything else done. When I was training for the Ironman, I asked Luc if he wanted to ride his bike alongside me as I pushed through the swimming, biking, and running parts of the competition. He felt incredibly valued on these long, hot runs because he knew that he was helping me achieve my goal. After I finished the Ironman, I often reminded him how important it was to have him ride alongside me and how grateful I was for his support and encouragement.

Matthew 6:21 says, "For where your treasure is, there your heart will be also." When I made the chart so I could understand how I spent my time, I discovered what my true treasure was: I was pouring my heart into my work. I had filled my days and nights with work, meetings, calls, business dinners, and travel.

When I began scheduling regular time with each of my kids—making them my priority—and scheduled everything else around them, I made my wife and my children my treasures. I literally awakened to my treasures.

Some men never realize how much they treasure their family. Others make the discovery through a personal health or life crisis that exposes the fragility and importance of these relationships. That doesn't have to be you.

> Some men never realize how much they treasure their family. Others make the discovery through a personal health or life crisis that exposes the fragility and importance of these relationships.

I'm determined to make sure that my family knows I value them—and that they know I've prioritized my time with them. But the outcome sometimes is not what I intended. Let me give you an example.

One Saturday, I planned a memory-lane date with Megan, filled with activities from running with her to going to a peach festival to having dinner out and a nightcap back at home. Throughout the day, I planned to enjoy thumbing through several family photo albums with Megan. Grace agreed to watch Luc and Zoey so Megan and I could have our memory-lane date.

Long story short, we wound up including the kids at several points, and I forgot the albums! Nonetheless, Megan appreciated my efforts in planning that day and loved the new memories we created.

I received an extra bonus from Grace. Her text exchange with one of her friends helped me realize how important it is that my actions reflect how a man should treat his wife and how a father loves the mother of their children.

> GRACE: Babysitting my sibs while my dad takes my mom on a "memory lane" date

> FRIEND: Awe That's cute ☺

> GRACE: Ikr! Relationship goals: find me a man who will plan dates for the entire day and actually tries.

When you plan special times with your kids, figure out when they are the most receptive. You wouldn't want to take your night owl on a sunrise date, for example. And be sure to avoid things they don't like—for example, a certain day or time, or a certain setting. No one feels valued when forced into a situation they don't like.

Elasticity

Elasticity refers to stretching your time, so you can create moments from events that already involve you. Do chores with your kids, invite them to join you on your errands, or serve together in a mission. Don't let what you have or haven't done in the past limit you. Get creative!

Grace likes for us to talk in the car on our twenty-minute drive home after choir practice. One evening I asked her, "What's your favorite song that your choir is learning?"

"It's an American folk song: Oh, Shenandoah!" she said. "It's the story of a canoe-going trader who loves Chief Shenandoah's daughter and wants to marry her!"

When we got home, we sat in the driveway another thirty minutes, talking about other songs and their origins. I've had similar conversations with Grace many times since then. We've covered topics from her views on the presidential candidates to what she'd do if she were president, from the latest article in her high school newspaper (yes, you should pick one up and read it each month), to the most interesting TED talks I've heard.

"I listened to a TED talk today that made me think of you," I said, handing Grace my phone. "Take a quick listen."

The talk was by a woman who described her views on feminism and equal rights for women and men. I knew that Grace was passionate about feminism.

"What do you think?" I asked.

"Interesting. I kind of agree with her," she said.

The first time Grace had asked me what feminism was all about, I gave her a flip answer and said something like, "women feeling more valued." I wasn't trying to be disrespectful, but I didn't understand how important the issue was to her then. Now we were sharing a short video and talking about it.

What began as routine trips to pick up Grace from choir has turned into some of our most important moments together— opportunities for me to show that I value both Grace and her opinions. Perhaps it's because we're fully present without distractions, or maybe it's the "talking through the windshield" that makes the discussions more comfortable. Whatever it is, I want more.

One evening, I asked Luc, a morning person like me, if he wanted to come with me on my run the next day. He was excited to be invited, and the next morning he was up and ready well before I was. After the first mile, however, he felt winded and wanted to stop. I have to admit that my response was frustration, and Luc felt the brunt of my disappointment.

A few days later, I changed my perspective completely. An older friend told me that whenever his son had asked him to play ball or to do something else together, he'd always said "yes" and dropped everything to spend time with him. Something inside me changed that day.

Luc and I were both still stinging from the emotional separation we felt, and I wanted to smooth things over. When I got home that night, I went upstairs and knocked on his door.

"Got a minute?" I asked.

"Sure," Luc replied. "Come on in."

"Listen, buddy. I'm really sorry for getting angry during our run earlier this week. I really want to spend time with you, and I was being selfish. Can you forgive me?"

"No problem, Dad. I forgive you," Luc said graciously.

"Can we try it again next week—to go for a run or walk? I'd like us to have some time together," I said.

The next week, we went on another morning run. But this time, when Luc wanted to take a break and walk for a bit, we did. It was my chance to hear about what was going on at school and with his friends. In only a few short years, he'll want to run faster and farther, and his old man will be the one who needs a break! Now, I see this time together as the gift it truly is.

Sometimes you'll discover elasticity in your schedule quite by accident, as I did. When Luc was younger, I drove him to dance practice every Monday. Zoey was eight at the time and too young to stay home alone, so she came with us. At first, Zoey and I each brought something to read while we waited the hour for Luc. But one week, we drove to a nearby park and played basketball and wiffle ball, and swung on the swings before it was time to go back for Luc.

The next week, Zoey suggested that we bring our gloves and a softball so she could practice pitching. Thanks to this extra hour for Zoey to practice in subsequent weeks, she was the star pitcher of her team in her first year of kid-pitch softball.

Be on the watch for elasticity in your schedule so you can easily transform a duty or chore into a real and valued moment with your child.

Ideas to Implement

To plan your individual time with your kids, first step back and observe when your child is most available, when he or she is most responsive to dialogue and open-ended questions, and when your child shuts down to ideas or questions. Then try some of these strategies to create shared experiences that fit your children's schedules and take into account when their hearts and minds are most open:

- When you're with them, be fully present, fully listening, fully focused on him or her at that time.

- When you're about to leave for a shared experience with your child, let him or her see that you're leaving your phone behind. This action will be a tangible sign that your priority during your time together will be your child above anything or anyone else.

- Make a regular date day with each of your children for adventure time, and plan a day of discovery together.

- Forego one of your scheduled items this week to surprise your kids with a spontaneous outing together or heart-to-heart talk.

- Keep your eyes open for fun opportunities to share experiences with your kids. Direct mail, blast emails, the local news on TV, and the daily newspaper are all sources to tap for great times together. One day I mistakenly opened a junk email that offered a tour of a potato chip factory. Wow! This could spell adventure in our house!

WHAT IS REQUIRED OF ME?

Time is perhaps life's most precious commodity, and what you choose to do with it can help your child feel loved, valued, and known—or not.

To make each child a priority, you'll have to become much more intentional with your time and take greater control of how you spend it. You'll also have to give up much of your alone time. But the priceless payoffs are that you'll move from being a tourist in your own life to being a full-in, full-on participant; and your child will gain the self-confidence and self-esteem that come from feeling truly valued.

CHAPTER 8

◆

There's never a good time to talk to my kids.

One afternoon, I got home early and was able to pick up Grace after school. I was in a great mood and couldn't wait to share the beautiful day with her. I pulled into the pick-up lane and saw her immediately. Grace saw me, too, but dropped back into her phone to read her latest Snapchat or Instagram post. She got in the car, and we exchanged a quick "hi."

"How'd your day go, Grace?" I asked.

"Fine," she replied mechanically.

"What time is choir practice tonight?" I asked.

"Same as always," she shot back.

"How much homework do you have tonight?"

"A lot."

"Do you need help with anything?"

"Can we talk about this later?" she said, returning to her phone, and clicking, swiping, and liking away.

So much for sharing this beautiful day and my great mood with Grace.

At the time, I was convinced that there just was never a good time to talk to my children. But since then, I've learned that the solution—the *only* solution—is to find a time that works best for *them* and then to adjust your schedule to match it. It may sound simple, but the execution is often difficult.

Grace and I had been in the car together, but I was in my own world and she was in hers. After a long day in class, working on assignments in study hall, and on social media with her friends, she needed a break.

I thought I was being sociable by making conversation and offering to help with her homework, but she felt pressured by my inquiries. I saw her stress, and it said, "I need a break."

> One of the best ways to make your children feel valued is to make *your* time *their* time *whenever* the situation arises.

I no longer talk to Grace about her schedule or logistics or homework right after school. I give her forty-five minutes to unwind, and after that she tells me her plans for getting her homework done and asks for help if she'll need it.

You've doubtlessly been interrupted by your children when you were doing something you wanted to do—reading a book, watching a show, or working on a project, for example. Maybe you got a little angry or felt impatient because you wanted what you wanted—uninterrupted time to do what you needed or wanted to do.

We all know what this feels like, but we also have to remember that our kids know what these moments feel like, too, and how we handle them makes a big impression—either positive or negative. One of the best ways to make your children feel valued is to make *your* time *their* time *whenever* the situation arises.

Sounds impractical, doesn't it? I agree, but it's not impossible.

When you give your child this kind of attention, you demonstrate that *they're* the priority in your life, not your work, not your project, not your TV show, not your phone, not your general busyness. Do I suggest that you drop everything every time? I do. Stop *everything* so you can listen to them, even if it means you have to stay up late to finish what you were doing. If you absolutely cannot do this, then do the next best thing. Stop and listen to their request and set a time in the next hour to hear them out.

Just this morning, I planned to do some writing, and Zoey came in and asked me to help her practice her pitching. Her softball tryouts are this Saturday, and she wants to be the pitcher. My first reaction: "Go ask your brother or your mother."

I listened to her pitch the ball against the side of the house for awhile until I couldn't stand it any longer. I dropped my writing and went out to catch for her.

We're faced with choices like this every day and, yes, we *can* adjust our schedule to be available when the time is best for our kids. The benefit isn't that she will make the team or get better at softball. The real and lasting benefit is that she knows that I *value* what's important to her and that she's my priority. The question is, how do you find the right time for each of your kids?

FIND THEIR PRIME TIME

Open your eyes! When is your child the most talkative, most positive, most engaging, most happy or joyful? Think about what happened yesterday, then think about the past week, the past month, the past year! If you have trouble pinpointing their most receptive times, then do it the easy way. Ask them.

Grace is most open after choir practice. Luc's an early riser, and if I can catch him before a screen does, we connect about what projects he's working on at school or what skills he's practicing in baseball. For Zoey, playing a game with her tends to make her happy. After we spend some silly time together, we talk about her friends at school, her Brownie troop, or her sports.

You also need to know when they're the least engaging and the least happy. After prolonged periods of screen time, all my children are lethargic and at their lowest energy level. That's why I have to set boundaries around when and how long they can be on screens.

It's up to you to adjust your schedule so that you're available at their most engaging times.

SEIZE THE MOMENTS

Today the sun was out, there was a cool breeze, and a taste of spring showed itself in February. Once again, I found myself in the pick-up line at school. I could tell Grace wanted to talk by the smile on her face and song in her voice. She described an upcoming trip she was taking with a friend.

Since it's only a mile and a half from school to home, I pulled into a vacant parking lot to give us more time together. I listened to her talk about the upcoming trip.

"I rented a bunch of movies, like *Pride and Prejudice*—you know, the one with Keira Knightley!" she explained excitedly.

I didn't know that movie, but I listened intently.

"I also bought a whole bunch of healthy snacks, like the granola clusters from Whole Foods," she said.

"What do you plan to do on the trip?" I asked.

"We're going to spend time on the beach, play our ukuleles, and drink tea!" Grace answered.

Don't be so tight-fisted with your own agenda that you miss these beautiful times. Seize the moment! If you blast through opportunities like this, they'll be lost forever. These are times when you can affirm your children and build them up.

Another time, I was driving Grace to meet friends for ice cream after one of her choir concerts.

"You were amazing tonight," I said. "I know how hard you worked to learn how to sing jazz. It's so different from what you do in choir, and you nailed it!"

"Thanks! I was singing scat!" Grace explained.

"What's scat?" I asked.

"Scat is a freestyle type of jazz singing where you make sounds like *shooby-do-wop-boppity bop bop bop*," Grace sang.

"Well, you sounded like a natural. I'm proud of you for jumping in to a new style of music. You definitely have the talent!" I said.

"Thanks, Dad! I really love it!"

When I was a tourist in my own life, I used to miss these moments. I don't do that anymore. I wouldn't miss this joy for the world.

One day, I was on a long training run with Luc and he was riding his bike next to me. It was the perfect time to talk about baseball, his friends, and his dreams of becoming an actor and a teacher and a professional baseball player, and he told me about all of that. Because I was panting during the run, it was much easier for me to listen than talk!

If you listen to your kids when they're ready to talk, they know that they matter. They know that they are valued.

IDEAS TO IMPLEMENT

- Do you lead with an interrogation instead of listening actively and seeking to understand your kids? Be silent long enough to let them start talking first.

- Observe your kids and note when they're most receptive to you, as well as the times they're not. Stay away from their "off" times. Don't push yourself on them.

- Does your child misunderstand or mistrust your motives? Many times, as young people seek to establish their own identity independent of their parents, parental questions seem more like an inquiry rather than an expression of a true interest in them and their lives, interests, dreams, and fears. Try asking your kids what they think about things that are happening in the news to open up new conversations.

- Practice dropping everything to focus on your child. Next, practice doing it without irritation.

- Ask your child when is a good time to talk.

WHAT IS REQUIRED OF ME?

The bottom line is that it requires you to lay your life down for your kids. You have to stop putting yourself first, and that's never easy.

PART 3

Children Need to Feel *Loved*

What does it mean to be **LOVED**? Love often looks like an expression of feelings or emotions, but I think that's only part of it. A father's love is a *doing* love that leads to your child *feeling* loved.

Our ultimate example, of course, was when our Heavenly Father sent Jesus to die for us. Jesus became the way to God's love. I'm not asking you to sacrifice your child, but a father's love is sacrificial.

When have you felt most loved by your father? A father's love can take on many forms. Many times a father's love looks and feels like safety and security. Protection is a gift we can give our children that makes them feel loved. Knowing that "there is nothing you could ever do to make me love you less" is something every child should experience.

> Knowing that "there is nothing you could ever do to make me love you less" is something every child should experience.

There is something almost holy about a child falling into their father's arms. Whether it is after a difficult situation and a child needs a shoulder to cry on, or when a child can't see the outcome of their efforts and needs a shoulder to stand on, feeling a father's love is a great gift.

A father's love shows strength—strength to admit we're wrong, strength to be vulnerable and ask for forgiveness, and strength to ask for help. A father's love can be wisdom in the form of words of advice or encouragement, or in silent presence and listening. A father's love is sacrifice—sacrificing what you want to do to make sure your children feel loved. This is a father's greatest gift: to love.

CHAPTER 9

◆

I Don't Know What
Fatherly Love Looks Like.

The first time I remodeled a bathroom was in our first home in Michigan. I had to figure it out on my own—from bathroom fixtures to tiles to plumbing to electricity. Because I needed help in so many areas, I went to Home Depot and spoke with an expert who helped me put together a plan. Tub and shower, sinks, flooring, lighting—they all had to be measured and planned out on paper. Once the layout was designed, Megan and I could pick out the fixtures, materials, designs, and colors. We were off and running!

That's when I developed a formula that I still follow when I want to learn to do something: figure out what you don't know or want to learn, find experts who can help, and ask the experts for help.

FIGURE OUT WHAT YOU DON'T KNOW

So what if you don't know what fatherly love looks like? Maybe you grew up in a house where your father was absent due to divorce, illness, death, or travel. Perhaps you were a victim of physical or verbal abuse and, rather than learning about what a father's love looks like, you learned what it isn't.

My father was the strong, silent type who'd grown up in post-World War II New York, worked a lot, and had five kids. One-on-one time with Dad was limited. And Dad wasn't a big communicator, but I knew he loved me. Even so, I didn't have a strong sense of how to model fatherly love to my children.

> That's what fatherly love looks like. It's showing your children that there's *nothing* they could do that would make you love them any less.

I found the perfect model in the story of the Prodigal Son. You remember that parable, don't you? A father had two sons, one of whom claimed his inheritance early but was so irresponsible that he spent it all in a frivolous spree. Broke and hungry, he could only find work slopping the pigs at a local farm. After awhile, he decided to return to his father's home to beg for work as a hired hand because he knew how well his father treated his workers.

But that's not how it worked out. As soon as the father saw his son coming down the road, he ran straight to him, embraced him, and welcomed him home. He butchered the finest calf in celebration that his son, who had been lost, was found.

That's what fatherly love looks like. It's showing your children that there's *nothing* they could do that would make you love them any less. That's to say that a father's love isn't earned and it isn't deserved; it just *is*.

You might feel pretty certain that your kids know that you love them, but are you sure they know they can't *lose* your love? Every child longs to hear these words, and every father can make it a habit to say them often: There's nothing you could ever do to make me love you less.

Just as I needed help to become a loving parent, to know what fatherly love looks like, and to learn how to tell my children that I love them *unconditionally*, you may as well.

FIND EXPERTS WHO CAN HELP

As men, we're wired for adventure. Facing adversity is part of any great adventure, and sharing the parenting experience with other fathers offers you friendships for a lifetime.

At the same time, admitting that you need help in being a better father can be quite humbling in a world where we're told that knowledge is power. That may well be true, but I believe relationships are even more powerful than knowledge.

Do you know a great father who raised kids who are secure? Do you have a spiritual mentor who can help you learn what fatherly love looks like? Find a guy—a pastor, an accountability partner, a neighbor, a relative—with whom you can share your successes and failures, your needs and shortcomings, and who can encourage you as you encourage him. If you're not already part of a church or a men's group, I suggest that you find one that feels right and fits where you are on your faith journey.

When we moved to our home in Saint Louis, I seriously questioned myself. How could I handle a job that demanded that I travel overseas once or twice a month and still be a good husband and father, as well as the spiritual leader of our family? I knew I needed help.

First, I went to our pastor. I told him I wanted to connect with other men in the congregation who were in the same phase of life as me, so we could share the journey of being husbands and fathers together. He told me there was no such group and encouraged me to form one.

"Padre" gave me the names of twelve guys who were in a similar stage of life and invited them to meet at my house for twelve weeks. The first week, my family and I were out of town, but the group met in our basement. The second week, I was in China on business, but the men met in our basement again.

The third week, I was in town, eager for my first meeting. Luc answered the door and showed the guys the way to the basement, where I waited for them.

"Oh, you're the guy who lives here!" one of them said.

At this meeting and the nine that followed, this group of men became my lifelong friends. And when the twelve weeks were over, with Padre's direction, I launched a men's Bible study to keep me accountable. It was actually more like a Christian book club since I didn't have enough Bible knowledge to run a study.

We announced the first meeting in the church bulletin. The plan was to meet weekly in a local coffee shop. The first week, I went to the coffee shop and sat by myself, discouraged that nobody else was interested enough to come. *Maybe this isn't God's plan.*

The second week, I read the devotional by myself, and I did the same thing the next two weeks. It finally dawned on me that if I didn't want to sit by myself every week, I had to personally invite other men and get their commitment to come. That approach worked, and now our group of twelve to fifteen men meets every Friday morning at six thirty. Many of us also do service projects together, along with our sons.

We've studied together, and we've shared our personal experiences at great length. Our collective knowledge and skills made *the group* the expert; and when we discussed our successes and failures, our fears and our foibles, our collective advice provided the direction we needed. From these men, from this group, I've learned how to be a better husband and father.

ASK THE EXPERTS FOR HELP

What is an expert, after all? An expert is simply someone who has knowledge or skill in a specific area.

If you can't find a group to discuss parenting or to learn more about issues such as discipline, boundaries, communication, trust, and responsibility, start one. Together, you can discover tools—like the love languages—and techniques—such as active listening—to equip you to be the best possible father. Your group will become a support team that encourages each member and holds each of you accountable to make your wife and kids your top priority.

One member of our group told us that he struggled to relate to his daughter and longed for a closer bond with her. We encouraged him to set aside some father–daughter time every week and to tell his daughter that he wants to know her and wants her to know how important she is to him. We continue to encourage him, and he gives us regular updates on his progress.

When I finally realized that Grace was suffering from anxiety and depression, I blamed myself. But when I shared my problem with a friend in our group, he asked, "What would you do if, God forbid, if you found out that Grace had multiple sclerosis?"

"I would get her the best help possible," I said, "and then educate myself as best as I could to support her.

That's what I needed to do—get Grace the best help I could and educate myself about her condition. We tried out a behavioral medicine group and a couple of counselors before Grace found one she liked. I immediately registered for a program at a local high school about teens and anxiety, and Megan and I both attended. From that point forward, we were all in.

Love Isn't Lost

You may be pretty certain that your kids know that you love them, but do they know they can't lose your love? Your kids long to hear these words, and you can make it a habit to say them: "There's nothing you could ever do to make me love you less." I had to learn this.

"Luc, are you on the iPad?" I asked as I entered the living room. "I specifically said that you had lost your privileges today because you didn't do what you were told yesterday."

"I forgot," Luc replied sheepishly.

"That's no excuse. You don't care and don't respect what I told you." I started to raise my voice. "Put the iPad down and go to your room, NOW!" Not one of my best parenting moments.

As dinnertime neared, Luc was still up in his room. I went upstairs to get him for dinner and thought, *He needs to apologize to me for disobeying,* and I was going to make sure he did. But when I opened his door, he was lying under the bed covers, completely covered up.

I pulled back the covers, saw my sweaty little boy underneath, and looked in his eyes and said, "I'm really sorry for yelling at you. I overreacted. Can you forgive me?"

Luc looked at me and said, "I forgive you, Dad, and I'm sorry I disobeyed you."

In that moment of failed fatherhood, my son saw my humanness and we connected deeply.

"I forgive you, buddy," I said. "There's nothing you could ever do to make me love you less."

That's what fatherly love looks like. It looks like failure, apology, and forgiveness.

PRACTICE THE ORDER OF LOVE

I'm sure you've heard that "love is patient, love is kind." It's a verse from the Bible, and it's a favorite to read at weddings because it gives us a picture of what love really looks like.

Take note of the order of love. Love is patient before all things. Patience requires us to listen, to seek forgiveness, and to diffuse negative situations with our kids—which in turn creates space for love to be kind. Kindness means that we perform acts of love toward our children, for example, when we help them with something they're struggling with, offer an encouraging word, and support their dreams.

This biblical picture of love shows that love is not a feeling; it's an action. *Feeling* love is emotional, like how you felt when you first dated your wife or first held your child in your arms. It's a warm and wonderful feeling. *Doing* love means action, like sacrificing your personal time and priorities for your children.

When I first met my wife, I felt excited and nervous—and I sensed a new adventure was dawning. Swept away in my feelings for Megan in those first weeks and months, I'd do anything for my love. *Doing* love early in our relationship was easy: it was new and fresh, and it was my top priority to feel good.

When Megan and I got married, had children, and bought a house, I worked at my job and had community responsibilities on top of my own interests. With competing priorities, *doing* love was much more of a sacrifice for me than before. For example, I had to choose not to hang out with my friends at a ballgame so I could be at my mother-in-law's birthday dinner. I did this because I loved my wife, and it made her happy to see her mother happy.

When I *do* love with our kids, I might have to give up a workout or a TV program to join them on a walk or watch a movie or TV show that they like. This type of sacrificial love demonstrates to my kids that they're deeply loved, and as their father, it's incredibly important to me that they know that.

IDEAS TO IMPLEMENT

- Read up, seek experts, and ask others to share their experiences, experts, or sources of information.

- Join the men's group at your local church. Ask the pastor for information or go to the website and contact the men's group leaders directly.

- Find out if there's a Christian businessmen's group in your city that you could join to meet other fathers on this journey.

- Identify leaders in your social circles who may have expertise, or at least some relevant experience, in the areas of parenting where you feel most challenged.

- Talk to a friend about how your struggles with your child.

  - Do they have a child of similar age or interests, or are they a few years ahead?

- Do they know anyone else who has faced similar challenges?

What Is Required of Me?

You've started learning what fatherly love looks like because you're reading this book. But learning more about it needs to become a priority. Find an expert and get their advice—and be

> No matter what your children do or don't do, it's essential that you let them know that you love them.

humble enough to share that you don't know what to do.

Don't be that guy who's lost and won't ask for directions or look at a map. Now is the time to ask for directions, particularly if fatherly love isn't something you experienced yourself. Talk to other dads and reach out to someone and ask for help.

Above all, understand that you'll be required to try a lot of new things: new words, new actions, new feelings. Think of it as an adventure, and make a plan to get started today.

No matter what your children do or don't do, it's essential that you let them know that you love them. Even if your child strikes out in softball, gets a C or worse on a test, doesn't turn in a homework assignment (or several assignments), disregards a family rule, or breaks some of your favorite tools or gadgets, tell your child that you still love him and always will—no matter what. No child should live in fear of losing your fatherly love. Make sure your children *see* it, *feel* it, and can *count* on it.

CHAPTER 10

◆

I'm Not a Touchy-Feely Guy.

Are you macho too mucho? The word *macho* indicates a masculine pride, or being manly. The word emerged in the United States around 1925. It originated in Spain and Portugal and referred to the ideal characteristics of men at that time— assertive, virile, and dominant.

Obviously, the male ideal has changed since then, which has created confusion. Sometimes I don't know what role I'm expected to play. What I do know is that I'm not as sensitive as I could be, I don't like to apologize or seek forgiveness, and I'm not good at being vulnerable.

My love language is touch, which stems from growing up in a big Irish Catholic family where barrel-chested uncles bear-hugged all their nieces and nephews. I'm a touchy-feely guy, but maybe you aren't.

It's like the story of the fajita I heard from a second-generation Mexican-American friend. Fajitas are a delicious Mexican meal made of sizzling meats and peppers, served with tortillas and toppings on a metal griddle. The meat for fajitas is always the choicest cut of beef, the most tender and flavorful. But if you're a butcher in Mexico, you don't take the choice cuts for yourself. You sell them to your customers at a premium. What's left behind is the beef shank, the cut of beef at the shin and legs of the cow, which is dry, tough, and sinewy. That's what you take home to your family.

But what man wants to serve his family the toughest cut of beef? So the butcher marinates the beef shank for twenty-four to forty-eight hours to make it moist, tender, and flavorful. He then presents his family with a delicious meal made from a cut of meat that he hand-crafted to please them. The butcher has turned something tough into something tender and has poured his love for his family into the shank to serve the best to them.

Like the butcher, we must be creative and turn something tough into something tender. If we want to give our families the best we have to offer, we need to turn our old ways into new ways.

When Grace was nine months old, my wife's friend suggested that we use sign language to communicate with her. I thought this sounded a bit hokey, but Megan wanted to try it.

When Grace was hungry or thirsty, she expressed her anger the only way she could: she cried louder and louder and LOUDER! When she wasn't crying, she would throw things. So we thought we'd give sign language a try.

The first thing we learned was the sign for *food*. We pulled our fingertips together and motioned toward our mouths. As we did this, we said "food, food" to teach her what that sign meant.

Soon Grace started to make that sign when she was hungry. So with that success under our belts, we taught her the sign for *drink*, which was squeezing your fist, and even got her to sign *more, please*, and *thank you*.

It felt a little bit like training a dog to do tricks. But the best part was that once Grace learned to communicate with us, she threw fewer toys, and there were less tears and tantrums. This experience showed me the importance of teaching our kids to put their needs into words.

It's the same thing with their feelings. Children need to feel free to communicate those as well. But I'm a guy, and I was raised to suppress my feelings, not express them, so at first this felt uncomfortable. My father was a man of few words who rarely expressed his feelings. I knew he wasn't happy when he yelled at me, so I tried not to make him angry, and we kids pretty much did whatever Dad said.

That kind of dictatorship hasn't continued in my home. In fact, I rarely feel like my children do what I say. I once asked a therapist friend why it's so hard to get my kids to do something I ask them to do, simply out of respect and honor for me. She busted out with a full belly laugh. Apparently that's not the way it works anymore. Because I want to build a different kind relationship with my children, I have to consider their feelings.

Does that mean that we dads need to become touchy-feely, all sensitive and vulnerable, for our kids to know they're loved? Not necessarily. But it does mean that to connect with them on a deeper level, we need to better understand both ourselves and them. If touchy-feely means becoming more sensitive to the needs of your kids and often doing things that you don't like to do—like asking for forgiveness—then yes, you're going to have to get touchy-feely.

If you want *them* to be forgiving and understanding, *you* have to model what forgiveness and understanding mean. To do these things, you must lead with your heart, so that *your* heart can lead *theirs*. You must train yourself, be transparent, be vulnerable, and serve others.

TRAIN YOURSELF

Start by trying to connect with the child in you. I know what you're thinking: "Don't start on that inner-child stuff!" It's important to start with yourself, so you can relate to where your children are now. You certainly had strong feelings as a child. Think back to the times when you were happiest, saddest, most angry, or most remorseful. Immerse yourself in the memories, and remember what it was like to *feel* as a child.

As I immerse myself in my memories, I remember the freedom I felt the year I got a bicycle for Christmas. I could ride really far away from home and be gone the whole day. I felt a whole new level of adventure.

I remember when I saw a neighbor boy get hit by a car. His white T-shirt was blood-stained when the ambulance came and took him away.

I remember visiting my older brother in the hospital after he'd had surgery to remove his brain tumor. The sight of all those black stitches, contrasted against his shaved head, struck fear in my heart.

I also remember that our house smelled like pasta on Wednesdays, when my mom cooked our family dinner, and that we all sat down for a meal when Dad came home from work.

I remember Sunday afternoon dinners with our family at two o'clock or three o'clock in the afternoon and thinking how great it was! I still have a dining room set from my parents. Oh, how I long for more family meals together! I want my children to feel that same sense of family and of safe, secure love surrounded by the tastes and smells of delicious food and laughter.

When I got older, my most angry time was when I lost my father the year after I graduated college. I'd just received my engineering degree and started a new job. I was proud to drive my new car home to show it off to Dad, and I looked forward to the two of us having some fun together.

Dad said to Mom, "Look, honey, he's driving a nicer car than I am!"

There was just the right mix of joy and envy to let me know how proud Dad was of me for getting off to a great start in life.

One night back at my apartment in Ohio, the phone rang. Mom told me through broken tears that Dad had had a heart attack and died while they were away on a trip. I stood there, stunned, unable to process what I'd heard.

I drove home for the funeral service and saw all my siblings, along with my aunts and uncles, cousins and friends. After the funeral, I walked through the cemetery and screamed at the top of my lungs, "Why? Why?" I was very mad at God that my father had died.

Dad's dream was to send all five of his children to college, which he did. He never went to college himself, and I realized what a sacrifice he'd made so I could have a better life. The deep pain I felt at his death, coupled with my dad's example of sacrifice, was a turning point in my life. I resolved to lead my life to positively impact others, not simply to please myself.

The next spring, I decided to serve in the Big Brothers/Big Sisters organization, which matches up young boys and girls, most being raised by a single parent, with older brother or sister figures. When I was accepted into the program, I learned that my "Little" was named Michael. I was stunned because that was my father's name. From then on, whenever someone asks me why I do the things I do, I answer, "Because it has been done for me."

Three of my happiest moments were the births of each of our three children. I remember the doctor who delivered Grace walking into the delivery room and asking, "Is she deliverable?" I remember Luc's surreal birth in a quiet hospital room in Belgium, with songs by the Irish singer/songwriter Enya playing in the background. And I remember Zoey bursting into the world in a new hospital wing in Saint Louis. Each of these treasures is a story of undeserved blessings that changed me forever.

One of the holiest moments in my life was in January 2016, when I joined a friend on a mission trip to Guatemala, and we brought new shoes and school supplies to the children. We played games and shared stories; and we washed the feet of these children ages nine to seventeen, placed new socks and shoes on them, and prayed together.

One fifteen-year-old young man named Mercado asked me in Spanish, "Why are you doing this?" As my interpreter shared Mercado's courageous question, I felt dumbstruck and wondered how I'd even gotten to this time and place.

I simply replied, "Because it has been done for me."

When I stopped thinking about myself, I received a precious gift. Through all of these experiences, whether as a child or as an adult, it has been by being humble and vulnerable through acts of service that I am able to get in touch with my feelings and, more importantly, understand my role as a father.

We need to train ourselves to communicate in ways that make our children feel loved. Grace's love language is words of affirmation, and I remember how hard it was at first for me to tell her what I appreciated about her. That was too touchy-feely for me.

It was particularly hard because I usually needed her to do something like empty the dishwasher or get in the car for school, and I felt disrespected because she wasn't cooperating. The last thing I wanted to do was compliment her, but I trained myself to do it.

> We need to train ourselves to communicate in ways that make our children feel loved.

When I finally surrendered to the fact that it was not about me and getting what I wanted, I opened up to finding new ways to reach her.

"I really like that jacket on you. It brings out the blue in your eyes."

"Thanks for helping clean up tonight."

Simple words of affirmation are how my daughter Grace knows she is loved

It was also hard for me to learn when to keep quiet and simply be with my children without giving them any instructions. I now look forward to my walks with my artistic daughter, who even grabs my hand and holds it every now and then.

BE TRANSPARENT

It was many years after my father's death before I realized that the anger that I felt so strongly stemmed from my own selfishness. I was mad that he'd died when I was barely out of college because I wouldn't be able to share golf and fishing weekends with him. And with this realization came my understanding of what his ultimate gift—his sacrificial love that had led him to educate all five of his children—meant to me.

When I shared this story over a cup of tea with Grace one November evening, I finally realized the full power of his ultimate gift. Even though I ached that she hadn't been able to meet her Grandpa Daniels, he lived on through me. Because he had modeled sacrificial love to me, I could now offer that to Grace.

I told Grace that my dream for her was that she know and love and serve God and others, exactly as God has planned for her. I longed for her to know that she was God's precious gift to me, and that I cherished her exactly as God made her.

"There is nothing you could ever do, Grace, to make me love you less."

BE VULNERABLE

Most people wouldn't describe me as humble. I am incredibly grateful, but humility is not my first nature. When I washed the feet of young children in Guatemala, I looked into their faces as they giggled. I was in a unique setting and felt quite vulnerable. Since it was my first time, I wondered if I was doing things right. Was I making the kids feel as silly as I looked? But that was the place where I shed all my selfish interests and became fully present to serve someone else. I finally understood the word *vulnerable*.

When Grace told me how angry she was that we didn't know she was suffering from anxiety and depression, I felt vulnerable then, too—vulnerable that I didn't have all the answers and vulnerable that I'd failed my daughter in her time of need. But we don't have to stay there. Feeling raw and vulnerable is a pathway to integrate a new learning into our own soul. From there, we can ask for forgiveness; continue to serve others through the mess; and reach the other side stronger, closer to those around us, and with a new understanding that we, too, are loved and valued.

SERVE OTHERS

Every year, we travel out East to visit family for Thanksgiving. We also try to find ways to be thankful and to serve others. It could be as simple as buying coffee for the next person in line or delivering a small gift to someone who has to work during the holidays.

One year, our family took up almost the entire airplane row on our return flight to Saint Louis. There were six seats across, and the Bean Team filled five of them. An unsuspecting young woman named Bethany sat in the sixth seat. Megan and Zoey started a conversation with her and found out that she was on a temporary assignment in Saint Louis.

After this meeting, we "adopted" Bethany into our family. She often came over for a movie or for game night, and she even attended some of the kids' performances. This became a model of love that our children not only observed but participated in, and they can't wait for Bethany's next visit!

It's important to find ways to serve others together. It doesn't have to be difficult. Just be observant, and when you see a need, fill it. Keep it simple, and you may gain a new friend along the way.

IDEAS TO IMPLEMENT

- Years ago, I started writing little supportive notes on the mirror in the kids' bathroom with a dry erase marker to encourage them in things large and small. We call these messages Mirror Me's. Examples are "Good luck on your AP history test today" or "I'm praying for you and your progress on your science project." Simple words of affirmation, such as "You're beautiful!" or "Be a light to others today!" can give your children a great start to their day and remind them about what's truly important in life. Now, as well as writing messages to Megan and me, the kids write Mirror Me's to each other, which has opened up a new line of communication between them and enhanced their sibling relationships.

- Make your child's lunch or snack for the day and drop in a warm-and-fuzzy handwritten note. The more specific the note, the better. But be sure to talk with your children after the first note to be sure that they aren't getting teased because of them. I've found that after writing so many notes to the kids over the years, it's gotten much easier for me to talk to them about what I think and how I feel about them.

- When the kids were young, we asked them to write down the things they liked to do on individual pieces of paper, which we folded and put in a jar. When we were trying to find a fun activity to do as a family, we pulled out one of the small folded papers and did that activity. These papers were like family fortune cookies—we never knew what was inside. We all agreed to do whatever the paper said, even if it wasn't our favorite. This "game" became an excellent lesson in sacrifice, in being part of a team, and in finding enjoyment in every opportunity to be together as a family.

WHAT IS REQUIRED OF ME?

Being touchy-feely is a good thing when it comes to having a better relationship with your children. The gift you give your children is the gift of your heart. How you express your thoughts and feelings toward them becomes their model for sharing their own thoughts and feelings. Most importantly, your words and actions show your children that they are loved.

By modeling your humility and vulnerability, your willingness to train your heart, and your humble service to others, you'll inspire your children in those same directions and communicate to them that they're loved. So jump in—and lead on.

CHAPTER 11

◆

I feel silly doing silly things.

Meet Zoeylicious, a princess who lives in Unicornlandia. Yes, Unicornlandia, the land of unicorns, where all day long, unicorns bounce from cloud to cloud and fly through rainbows. Zoeylicious has a beautiful unicorn named Kaitlyn, who is the fastest unicorn in all the land. Every night, Zoeylicious and Kaitlyn travel on a different rainbow color to a new place where they eat foods and enjoy drinks that are the same color. When they travel on a red rainbow, they eat apples, strawberries, and red Sour Patch Kids, and they drink fruit punch!

This adventure began one night when I was tucking Zoey, whom I often call Zoeylicious, in bed. She wanted me to read all her *Goldilicious* bedtime stories.

"But not with your sleepy voice," she said. Of course I had a sleepy voice! I was literally falling asleep while I read to her.

I asked, "Why don't you tell *me* a bedtime story tonight?"

On that night, Zoeylicious and Kaitlyn were born! The first story was fun, and each night after that we picked a new color of the rainbow to travel on. Then, the different foods and drinks that matched that color became part of our story. Eventually, I got my own unicorn named Pegasus. Apparently, carrying me around to all the colors of the rainbow slowed Kaitlyn down, and Zoeylicious didn't like that.

Zoey and I were so enthralled with our story that I hired a painter to paint rainbows and clouds all over her bedroom. Our silly adventures became the theme of her room.

With all your adult responsibilities and hectic schedule, it's not easy to be silly with your kids. After all, life seems pretty serious. But once you discover how much fun you can have by imagining together, being silly comes a lot more easily. And it's well worth trying, because silliness can be the start of an incredible bond with your child.

So how do you do it? Start small and start safe. Make up a new imaginary name or an imaginary pet. Create an imaginary hero and tell adventure stories about him or her when you're in the car or before your child goes to bed. Stir your child's imagination by asking fun questions: If you could have any superpower, what would it be and how would you use it? If you could paint or decorate your room in any way, what would it look like?

Don't be afraid to let your inner-child out to play. You may need him when you least expect it!

We went on a Disney cruise when Zoey was six months old, Luc was almost five, and Grace was seven. When our flight home was delayed—and the gate area was packed with tired, cranky families—memories of Mickey, Minnie, pirates, and princesses were fast forgotten.

There weren't enough seats for everyone in the gate area, so our family took over a patch of carpet on the floor and made camp for the long delay. It seemed the perfect time to get out the little finger puppets I always put in my travel bag to keep the kids happy on long flights. I pulled fifteen little finger puppets out of my bag, the kids each chose their favorites, and we took turns telling a story from the puppet's perspective.

The other kids in the gate area heard us and wanted to join in, so we expanded our circle to include ten more kids! After each child had told a puppet story, it was my turn to tell the final story. I pulled a gopher hand puppet from my bag and told my gopher story to each child's finger puppet in turn.

When I got to one of the three little piggies, I said, "What a fine brick house you have. You must be a master builder. But I'm a big gopher with a big appetite!"

My gopher smothered the piggy and made munching sounds as he ate him. The kids roared with laughter and asked for more. I, of course, complied.

When it was time to board the plane, one of the parents asked me, "Are you a teacher, or do you work with kids?"

"Some days I feel that way. No, I'm a business director at a major corporation. If my colleagues saw me right now, they wouldn't believe it was me!"

I was just a crazy dad who loved every adventure with my family.

Forget Your Reputation

You can have a moment like this if you're willing to put your ego aside and forget about what other people may think and the reputation you've tried to establish. Several years into my career,

I realized that my reputation at work had become too important to me and often snuffed out the crazy, silly father hidden

> You can have a moment
> like this if you're willing
> to put your ego aside and
> forget about what other
> people may think and the
> reputation you've tried to
> establish.

inside me. I wish I'd discovered
this earlier in my career, because
I missed many opportunities to
be silly with the kids. Now
we're always on the lookout for
crazy adventures. You can be,
too, if you stop taking yourself
so seriously.

One Christmas, I was four months into a new job as director of strategic initiatives. (Yes, that's a made up title!) When
people asked me what I did or what my title meant, I told them,
"I initiate strategery, of course!"

"What's strategery?" they asked.

"Exactly!" I replied, and we would break into laughter.

I used to take tremendous pride in my title and position, and
this flippancy was a nice change as I entered a season of adventure in a new job. Not only did I have fun with my job title, I
carried that whimsical attitude with me into the workplace.

We had an ugly sweater contest at my first Christmas office
party, and I wanted to do it up big. But we'd recently moved
into a new home, and I couldn't find my ugly sweater. I was
leaving on a business trip the next morning, so I asked Megan if
she'd pick up one for me at Goodwill.

I got home from my trip late that night, and the sweater
was sitting on the kitchen counter with two bags of chocolate
chips. I'd promised to bring chocolate chip cookies to work
for the party the next day and had hoped that one of the kids
would help me make them. Now that I didn't have any helpers,
I thought about running to the store to buy the slice-and-bake

version but decided against it. Instead, I pulled on the ugly sweater to see if it fit, preheated the oven, and jumped right into making cookies. A sleeveless thing, the sweater had a giant polar bear on the back; the front barely went down past my chest, exposing my midsection. It was a very weird sweater.

Midway through the cookie process, Grace came home. From the look on her face, I could tell she hadn't had a good day. I said hello to her, and she glanced at me as she walked past. It took a millisecond for her to process what she'd seen.

She stopped short, turned, gave me a Dad-has-lost-his-mind look, and asked, "What are you doing?"

I was wearing the crazy, lopsided sweater over my work clothes and was covered with blotches of flour and baking powder.

"What?" I said. "I'm making chocolate chip cookies!"

We shared a great laugh at my expense, and Grace left the kitchen with a smile. This moment of silliness helped lift her depression, and it felt good to be able to do that for her.

When I went to work the next morning, I got a lot of strange looks, as well as a couple of compliments about how ugly my sweater was. As it turned out, I was wearing a dog sweater, and when someone figured that out, we all roared with laughter!

I've discovered that when I forget about my reputation and lower my guard to have some fun at my own expense, it draws me closer to others—closer to my children, closer to my wife, and closer to my friends and colleagues.

AND YET, THERE IS A SERIOUS SIDE

Each stage of your child's life offers new adventures and is part of the journey from one season to the next. Both you and your kids can enjoy the adventures of the current season, while dreaming and hoping for what is yet to come. It would be foolish to pretend that life is all fun and games. There's plenty for your kids to be afraid of in this world, but you can help them turn those fears and uncertainties into dreams and possibilities.

Most kids have suffered from information overload from an early age. It comes from the media—the news, social media, and entertainment. Your kids don't have the skills or experience to put things in perspective, so they can develop deep fears about what they see and hear. When you balance negative or scary media messages with healthy doses of their dreams and the possibility of a bright and better future, you help them feel safe and secure. You also foster a climate where they feel free to ask questions about what they don't understand.

One way to do this is to use invitational language. Invitational language includes open-ended questions that give you the opportunity to listen: "What can I pray about for you today?" "How can I better support you this week/this semester?"

Another form of invitational language is to confirm that you understand what your child said by restating what you believe you heard: "So what you're saying is, you need me to give you more space after school to allow you time to unwind?"

A third type of invitational language is using second-level questions or requests that allow you to go deeper, gain a better understanding, and get to know your children better—while allowing your child to feel valued by being heard: "Tell me more about what you mean, so I can better understand."

We've already talked about active-listening techniques. When you choose words and ask questions that invite your children to share what they think and feel, you create a safe space for them.

If your children are young, ask them how something made them feel. Children are emotional beings, and most of what they take in from the world impacts their emotions. You can help them name their feelings to alleviate their frustration and allow them to process their experiences. By understanding their feelings, they'll be better able to show empathy and resolve conflict down the road.

One day, Zoey came home from school, clearly upset about something; but she didn't want to talk about it.

"Hey, Zo. You want to go shoot some hoops with me?" I asked.

"OK," came the less-than-enthusiastic response.

After we'd played a few minutes, I asked, "What happened today to make you upset?"

"Our teachers won't let us play kickball and throw the ball at the other players to get them out," she replied.

"Why is that?"

"Because they think it's mean, and some kids get hit in the head with the ball."

"How does that make you feel?"

"They treat us like babies!"

"I can see how that would make you upset," I said. "Is there anything you can do about it?"

"We could make a rule that if you hit someone in the head or too hard, you sit out that day," she suggested.

"That's a great idea. You should suggest that to your teacher," I said. "Please make sure you do it in a respectful way."

Hearing Zoey out helped me understand her immediate problem, know her better, and learn what makes her upset. When I asked questions, it helped her name her emotions and come up with ideas to improve the situation. In the end, she felt like she could have an impact on the situation, rather than be forced to simply accept something she believed wasn't right.

Another form of invitational language is to tell stories. Use a story from the news as the starting point, and ask your kids how they'd react in a similar situation. This can help them develop more mature thinking and prepare them for a time when they may face a similar situation.

I had a problem to solve in a training class I attended. I had to react to a scenario in which I was the coach of a baseball team made up of fifteen fourteen-year-old boys. The team had just won the state championship and would get an all-expenses-paid trip to the national championship. But only twelve players could suit up and go. Who would go and who would be left behind?

We discussed the problem as a family and bounced some ideas around. The discussion wasn't about coming up with one right answer. Instead, it was about how to explore our options and how to best decide who would play. The consensus was that if only twelve guys could play, and if we wanted to win the national championship, we had to choose the best players.

We talked about how it would feel to be left behind. One idea was to hold a fundraiser to pay for the benched players to go and cheer on their teammates. Another idea was to hold a special banquet at the end of the season, so all fifteen boys could celebrate the team's winning season and what they had accomplished together.

When you craft solutions together, you help your children build stronger values and character, even if they never experience the situation themselves. They become fortified to deal with their own disappointments and to respond to opportunities that come their way.

Don't wait for your children to fall into a pit before you build them up. Strengthen them before they reach that point, so they can draw on lessons learned when they need them.

IDEAS TO IMPLEMENT

- **Choose "our book."** Buy a book to read together and make it "our book." Pick one filled with adventure and wonder, and that sparks your child's imagination. You could even try "madlibbing" a fairy tale!

- **Go for drama.** Ask your kids what their favorite book or movie is, then reenact it as best you can. Of course, it will never go according to plan, and that's when it's fun to be silly and vulnerable with your kids. This is how you can grow into a new trust with your kids and build a relationship that says, "I want to love you, know you, and value you more than my reputation as a perfect or professional father."

- **Be their pathfinder.** Play the What Would You Do? game, where you share stories or scenarios with your kids, and then ask what they'd do in that situation. Don't judge their answers as right or wrong; instead, ask how they reached that particular answer. Example: Who would you invite to your birthday party if you could invite only eight kids? How would your other friends feel? What would you say when your friends who were left out asked why they weren't invited?

- **Share a situation from work.** Choose a work situation and share it with your children in a context they can understand. Seek their opinion and ask for their voice.

Start with some what if's. What if you were principal or president? What would you do in your first thirty days? Give me your acceptance speech.

What Is Required of Me?

Being silly means you have to be vulnerable—again! It also requires you to be creative. No going to acting classes! It's OK to feel silly when you're being silly. Get used to it!

Allow your kids to feel safe and secure to be themselves, and keep the lines of communication open. Being creative can help you express yourself as a parent who still has an imagination and dreams, and is still figuring things out. That's valuable for your kids to see.

In a time when pressure on kids is mounting and competition and performance is what it's all about, there are few safe places that are free from social media and inauthentic relationships. It's at home—where they are known, valued, and loved—that children can truly be themselves in full silliness and in full love.

EPILOGUE

The journey begins here, but it doesn't end here. Men long for adventure, and the journey of fatherhood is just that: an adventure! The road to making your child feel known, valued, and loved is full of sacrifices and tears, as well as extravagance and laughter. You may not have all the answers or the confidence or expertise in every situation, but commit to this journey anyway. This is your greatest gift and legacy.

I remember playing Pooh-stick—the game from the children's book, *Winnie-the-Pooh*, by A. A. Milne—with my children when they were young. The main characters—Winnie, Christopher Robin, Rabbit, and friends—all grabbed small sticks and stood atop a bridge that spanned a small creek. They dropped their sticks on one side of the bridge and watched them float down the creek and under the bridge on the other side.

That's exactly how we played it. I always tried to get my stick to go downstream the fastest without getting hung up in the branches, leaves, or rocks that stuck out of the water. As we watched our sticks start floating, they'd bump into these obstacles and rush through a narrow section, each stick taking its own circuitous path. We cheered our sticks on with shouts of joy and plenty of laughter.

Sometimes our family feels a bit like Pooh-sticks floating in the water. When one family member gets stuck or struggles, we lend a hand. When one member succeeds, we cheer. But along the journey, we're in it together, fully present. Sometimes, that is the greatest way our children can feel being known, valued, and loved.

My hope is that this book has both encouraged you and given you ideas to draw you and your children closer together in an authentic relationship. After all, why be a tourist in your own life when you can be a full-on, all-in participant alongside them?

May you be encouraged on your journey and seek your Heavenly Father, as well as other earthly fathers, to join and support you in this great adventure.

ABOUT THE AUTHOR

Rich Daniels is the husband of Megan Daniels and the father of their three children: Grace, Luc, and Zoey. A corporate entrepreneur with twenty-five years at Monsanto, Solutia, and Honeywell International and seven years in two start-ups, Rich finds his greatest purpose in bringing people together in community to serve others.

Although Rich has completed twenty-five marathons and two Ironmans, he relishes the endurance sport of fathering more than any athletic event. After forming a small men's group to share parenting experiences, Rich felt inspired to write a book to guide other men away from being tourists in their own lives and toward becoming involved, fully engaged dads.